READY...GO!

40 INSPIRATIONS FOR LIFE

JUDITH COX

READY…GO!

READY…GO!
40 Inspirations for life!

Copyright © 2024 by Judith Cox

All rights reserved. No portion of this book without permission may be reproduced, stored in a retrieval system, or transmitted in any form – scanned, electronic, photocopied or recorded without written consent of the author as it is strictly prohibited. Excerpts and links may be used, provided that full and clear credit is given to the author with specific direction and reference to the original content.

If you would like to use material from the book for short quotations or occasional page copying for personal or group study, this is permitted other than for review purposes. However, prior written permission must be obtained on request by emailing the author on judithmc07@outlook.com. All that is written in the book is solely the author's journey and experiences which can be used as quotes referenced clearly stated.

Unless otherwise indicated, scriptures are taken from the Holy Bible, New International Version. Copyright © 1973, 1978, 1984, International Bible Society. Used by permission of Zondervan Publishing House.

Scripture taken from the New King James Version. Copyright © 1982 by Thomas Nelson, Inc. Used by permission. All rights reserved.

Scripture quotations marked TPT are from The Passion Translation. Copyright © 2017, 2018 by Passion & Fire Ministries, Inc. Used by permission. All rights reserved. ThePassionTranslation.com.

Scripture taken from THE MESSAGE. Copyright © 1993, 1994, 1995, 1996, 2000, 2001, 2002. Used by permission of NavPress Publishing Group.

READY...GO!

Contents Page

Acknowledgements	1
Foreword by Pastor Stuart Bell	2
Introduction	3
Chapter 1: Transformation	6
Chapter 2: First Encounters	9
Chapter 3: God's Masterpiece	14
Chapter 4: Up, up, and Away!	17
Chapter 5: Orchestra on the Streets	20
Chapter 6: Playdough	22
Chapter 7: No Microwave Hatchings!	26
Chapter 8: First Glimpse of Dawn	29
Chapter 9: Daddy, do you see me?	32
Chapter 10: At the Woollen Mill	36
Chapter 11: Mountain Adventure	39
Chapter 12: A Beached Whale	43
Chapter 13: All Change!	46
Chapter 14: Crown Jewels	49
Chapter 15: Highway Maintenance	54
Chapter 16: Tagged for Blessing!	58
Chapter 17: Preparation is Key	61
Chapter 18: Amazing Grace	65
Chapter 19: Loss and Gain	68
Chapter 20: Remember Who you Are!	71
Chapter 21: Mum	75
Chapter 22: Full Steam Ahead!	78
Chapter 23: Tightrope Walk!	82
Chapter 24: Heart to Heart	85
Chapter 25: Wake Up!	88
Chapter 26: Raise the Flag!	92
Chapter 27: Do you hear the Drum Beat?	95
Chapter 28: Cry from the Heart	98
Chapter 29: A Mirage!	101
Chapter 30: The Way of the Lord	104
Chapter 31: Garden of Delights	107
Chapter 32: Sails to the Wind	110

READY…GO!

Chapter 33: Tent Pegs!   113
Chapter 34: Carry the Fire!   116
Chapter 35: Why do you lurk in the Shadows?   119
Chapter 36: Footprints in the Snow   122
Chapter 37: The River is Here!   125
Chapter 38: Dismantle   128
Chapter 39: A New Generation Rises   132
Chapter 40: Treasure to Share   135

Acknowledgements

Thank you to my lovely daughter; Katy, for helping with photography on the cover, and all things technical! You're a gem!

Thank you to all the children who have inspired and taught me through the years; many have now grown up with their own families!

I am grateful for you; the reader. May this book be a seed of blessing and inspiration to you and your family.

READY...GO!

Foreword

Over 40 years ago, Judith attended the church I was Pastoring. A number of teenagers gathered in our home, and a vision for the future was birthed. From those small seeds, a large strategic church emerged, together with a network of around 80 churches across the nation. Judith remains in one of our Alive Church locations, and has been a faithful member through the years. We have witnessed the power of Kingdom seeds over this period of time.

Judith's life is marked out by faithfulness and creativity. I am very happy to endorse her new book which speaks of seeds being sown, bringing Kingdom life and purpose.

Judith has drawn illustrations from her faithful walk with God, and has seen the life of the Kingdom in everyday activities, through the eye of faith. She has kept the Cross of Christ at the centre of her life, and it is from her personal walk with Christ that these life experiences have emanated.

My prayer is that every book will carry seeds of the Kingdom which will bring strength, encouragement, and challenge to everyone who reads.

Pastor Stuart Bell.

Founding Leader of the Ground Level Network of Churches, and Senior Pastor of Alive Church.

READY…GO!

Introduction

READY…GO! is birthed from a place of seeing Jesus in a vision. I see Him on the Cross, in the agonies of His last moments. He takes His final breath. As His head bows, a large sunflower is superimposed on the face of Jesus. Hundreds of seeds cascading down through the air from the middle of the flower head. I am deeply moved; it pierces my heart and powerfully radiates life and hope beyond the suffering and death. What a beautiful Saviour. I am captured by His amazing love. He pours out His life for me, for the world.

God sowed His Son Jesus, sacrificially, and reaped His reward. Jesus is the seed of Abraham.

"Now to Abraham and his seed were the promises made."

Galatians 3:16 (NKJV).

We are His reward, His seed, as we become united with Him. As a seed is buried, the husk of the seed falls away like an old cloak and starts to sprout new life!

"I tell you the truth, unless a kernel of wheat falls to the ground and dies, it remains only a single seed. But if it dies, it produces many seeds."

John 12:24 (NIV).

Jesus' death paved the way for the resurrection and new life. Three days later, He rose again and ascended into heaven where He now sits at the right hand of the Father. He is interceding for us, and preparing a place for us in Heaven! One day, He will return and receive those who have given their lives to Him. Christians believe faith in Jesus is the only way to Heaven. At 19 years old, I gave my life to God. His love was calling me to turn away from living for

READY...GO!

myself, to new life in Christ, and a purpose for living. A brand new, exciting adventure begins. I prayed something like this:

"Thank you, Jesus, that you love me and died on the Cross in my place for my sins. I believe that You God, raised Jesus from the dead, and I confess that He is Lord. I am sorry for the things I have done wrong. I turn from them to follow You. Please save me now; come into my heart and change me. I will love and serve you for as long as I live. Amen."

It is amazing to realise that I am a seed from this vision. The seed God plants in us will never be destroyed. My life is changed forever!

"For through the eternal and living Word of God, you have been born again. And this 'seed' that He planted within you can never be destroyed but will live and grow inside of you forever."

1 Peter 1:23 (TPT).

READY...GO! unfolds into 40 chapters of 'Inspirations for Life.' God speaks in our everyday lives. His Word of truth is illustrated in personal, real-life stories, dreams, visions and encounters with Jesus. He meets us where we are every day. Much of the book comes from journalling with the Lord and listening to His heart over a number of years. Here are seeds of hope for faith and a fruitful life.

Seeds are powerful and destinies will miraculously unfold, just as seeds have the power to break through concrete! God makes them grow! We become rooted in Him in the life-giving waters.

"As you therefore have received Christ Jesus the Lord, so walk in Him, rooted and built up in Him and established in the faith as you have been taught, abounding in it with thanksgiving."

Colossians 2:6-7 (NKJV).

I recall driving past fields of sunflowers in Southern France. It was an amazing sight as the bright yellow flowers reached to the sun. However, some flowers began to droop as in the vision, carrying an

READY...GO!

abundance of seeds! Each head can have one to two thousand seeds! That is a phenomenal multiplication!

At the end of each chapter, you are invited to write your own thoughts and reflections and seeds to sow.

"Whatever a man sows, that He will also reap."

Galatians 6:7 (NKJV).

There is power in every seed you sow to duplicate itself, multiply and produce a harvest. As we GO and share the Good News of the Gospel, the Word has power within it to save! Faith is a seed. Prayer and fasting are also seeds. In fact, we can sow generously and joyfully, whatever God has put in our hands. It may simply be a smile, a kind word or an encouragement. God has given each one of us gifts and talents we can sow into His Kingdom. The seed may be finances, prophecies, our work or time.

"Peacemakers who sow in peace reap a harvest of righteousness."

James 3:18 (NIV).

God invites us to step into a life-long adventure that requires courage and commitment. He calls us to arise in this generation, to be captivated by His love. Be revived! You will bring revival fire, the living flame burning within.

READY...GO!

READY...GO!

Chapter 1

Transformation

The awaited day comes. Great excitement and anticipation. A little scary too! Liz, an expert gardener arrives, armed with a spade, bucket, sacks, gloves and other gardening tools. My little garden is going to be radically transformed from its present unruly state! We make a start. First, the overgrown buddleia tree is reduced to a stump! Dozens of old flower pots dotted around the garden are collected. Many are cracked and split, and full of weeds!

A new day dawns; my garden is in good hands. We both sketched a garden design; they were amazingly similar! The work progresses. Clearing weeds, pulling up overgrown plants, keeping some for later planting. Everything is uprooted, apart from the buddleia stump and a honeysuckle bush. It is bare. It is bleak. It is messy. Nothing attractive, but now a blank canvas, ready for the work of art. Transformation begins!

The garden begins to takes shape. It can't be rushed. I have to be patient. The picture on the artists' easel comes to life. I watch as curvy borders are skilfully carved. A corner area at the bottom of the garden takes shape where I sometimes sit to catch the late afternoon summer sun! It is covered with pebbles. I lovingly call it my 'beach!' An old wooden palette, previously used as a guinea pig run, forms two raised beds for planting! An old wooden ladder sawn in half is positioned in each for climbers.

Then, a final work of art in the construction stages before planting begins. A wild idea, even a little scary I think at the time! The suggestion of a flower bed carved in a kidney shape in the middle of the lawn! It seems strange a few years later to think it was a scary idea. It turns out to be wondrous and unique, as I said, "Yes, go ahead!" Sometimes, change is hard, but I know I can trust an expert! The long process comes to an end after 9 months. The garden is

READY...GO!

complete and a joy to behold! Full of magnificent blooms, colours, and perfumes fill the air. A plan becomes a remarkable reality!

So too, God has His amazing plans for each of us. Real life lessons unfold. He is the Master Gardener. God created you! He loves you and knows you intimately. He has a unique plan for you. Firstly, that your heart is truly given over to Him as you turn from your old life, and enter in to all He has prepared for you. Jesus died on the Cross to pay for your sins so that you can know forgiveness and become a new person. The process of uprooting everything in the garden and breaking up compacted soil is brutal! It is those hard, painful and tough times in our lives that so often clear the way.

The Master Gardener comes to dismantle the old. Indeed, it is a scary, bewildering process sometimes, but as we yield to Him, He prepares the way for the new. Oh, so much better than anything you can imagine! He is trustworthy; He only wants the best for you. He is the restorer of life. He loves us enough to prune us; to make us more fruitful.

> **He transforms chaos into something beautiful and flourishing.**

"I am the true Vine, and my Father is the gardener. He cuts off every branch in me that bears no fruit, while every branch that does bear fruit, He prunes, so that it will be even more fruitful."

John 15:1-2 (NIV).

He cultivates and tills the soil of our hearts. Sometimes, it proves to be devastating and everything is laid bare, but it is worth it! I hear the Lord saying:

"I am excited about your transformation! I am with you. Through the Presence of the Holy Spirit, I am in you and working through you. You are being transformed by the renewing of your mind. I

READY...GO!

completely understand your situation. Yes, transitions are often painful, but know My amazing love and divine purpose for you. Feel My pleasure on your life."

God's first command to Adam and Eve is to *'be fruitful and multiply.'*

"So, God created man in His own image, in the image of God He created him, male and female He created them. Then, God blessed them and said to them, "Be fruitful and multiply; fill the earth and subdue it, have dominion over the fish of the sea, over the birds of the air, and over every living thing that moves on the earth."

Genesis 1:27-28 (NKJV).

God empowers us to establish His Kingdom on earth. As Christ reigns over creation, so in Him, we can achieve our original purpose; to *"be fruitful and multiply."* God has put you on this earth because He wants you here in this time. You have something this generation needs; a unique purpose. Don't diminish what you have. Fruitfulness flows from intimacy with God. As He transforms you, you bring transformation to others.

Activity: What areas are flourishing in the garden of your life? What needs attention? What seeds are you sowing?

_____
_____
_____
_____
_____
_____
_____

READY…GO!

Chapter 2

First Encounters

It is very late into the night. I listen to my little black portable radio under the bed covers! I was 13 years old then. I made sure my parents couldn't hear anything! A preacher on the Radio Bible Class spoke about Jesus and how much He loves me. He died for me and rose again, and He is alive today. I have not heard this Good News before and was drawn to listen to it many times late at night under the duvet! I began to question, "Why am I here on this earth? What is life about and what is the purpose?" I feel an emptiness and void inside. I have a deep hunger and thirst for truth…

My brother gave his life to God around that time and I began to see how God was changing him. We are not from a Christian family; however, I was sent to Sunday School at age 4 to a little church up the road near our house in Granborough, Buckinghamshire. The Vicar had been around the village promoting Sunday School. I expect my Mum and Dad were glad to stay at home on Sunday mornings for some peace! I remember colouring Bible story pictures and leaning on the back pew! We were given a stamp with a picture of Jesus on it each time we went. Even back then, I believe God was preparing my heart. Seeds were sown for an encounter with Jesus some years later.

Now ready to begin Teacher Training College in Lincoln, I travelled up from my home near Poole in September 1977. In my second year, I heard about Lincoln Free Church; a small church in a 'tin hut!' It sounds exciting! It was there that I found God's Presence in a very real and personal way for the first time. It touches my heart. I see people standing with eyes closed and arms in the air passionately worshipping God. I had never seen that before. It is real and I want to know more! They certainly seem to have something I didn't, or more realistically, they know Someone I didn't! On one particular Sunday, Stuart Bell; the Pastor, speaks about Peter from the Bible;

READY...GO!

how He follows Jesus *at a distance* near to the time of Jesus' death on the Cross.

"But Peter followed Him at a distance to the high priest's courtyard."

Matthew 26:58 (NKJV).

The sermon unfolded with this statement: We cannot "sit on the fence." That was definitely me! We are either "for" God or "against" Him. If we are *against* Him, then we might as well be shouting "crucify Him" along with the crowd at the crucifixion. It was black and white; a shocking thought as Jesus hangs there loving me. I am challenged to the core. He gave His life for me; how can I not give mine to Him? Jesus looks at Peter...

"And the Lord turned and looked at Peter. Then Peter remembered the word of the Lord, how He had said to Him, "Before the rooster crows, you will deny Me three times."

Luke 22:61 (NKJV).

Jesus' look of compassion pierced Peter's heart in that moment. I too, feel the loving eyes of Jesus locking gaze with mine. My heart melts. He is inviting me to repent and give my life to Him. I responded to the invitation of coming to the front of the church and gave my life wholeheartedly to Him. I prayed a similar prayer like the one in the introduction of this book. As I made my way to the front, the congregation started singing:

"I am coming, Lord, coming now to Thee,
Trusting only in the Blood that flows at Calvary."

It is a new beginning. We are born cut off from God because of our sin, but God the Father makes a way for us to come home through His Son. The Bible says *"For all have sinned and fall short of the glory of God."* Romans 3:23 (NKJV). This is the Good News:

READY...GO!

"Whoever calls on the Name of the Lord shall be saved." Romans 10:13 (NKJV)

The peace and joy is real. Jesus said on the Cross *"It is finished!" John 19:30 (NKJV)* He bows His head. The price for my freedom is paid in full. Many years later, God gives me the sunflower vision; the flower head superimposed on the face of Jesus. Seeds cascading down! I give Him all the thanks and praise.

"Therefore, if anyone is in Christ, he is a new creation; old things have passed away; behold, all things have become new."

2 Corinthians 5:17 (NKJV).

Many thanks and much appreciation to Stuart Bell, who has written the foreword for this book. I am very grateful for all God has done. When I completed my teacher training in Lincoln college, I wanted to stay in the city to be part of the church. I had no money, but God miraculously provided a job just for the last two weeks of term! I could put down a deposit for a bed-sit. Lincoln became my new home!

God opened the door for me to work at Sign of the Fish; a fish and chip shop set up by a newly saved businessman. While looking for teaching jobs, I had great fun serving fish and chips and was very grateful to God for His provision. I remember the joy of giving all my first week's wage into the Grapevine Celebration offering that year with a heart of gratitude!

Maybe you are ready to give Him your life for the first time? No more sitting on the fence. I thank God for His encounter with me at 19 years old. The God of heaven comes to dwell in me. It is a living vital relationship with a living God. An adventure begins! He gives me purpose for living where I previously felt empty and inadequate. I am chosen, loved, accepted, and He has plans for my future.

READY...GO!

"For I know the plans I have for you," declares the Lord, "plans to prosper you, and not to harm you, plans to give you hope and a future."

Jeremiah 29:11 (NKJV).

God has transformed my life. A journey from timidity to boldness; fear to courage. I love Him, and my passion is for others to know Him too. I have a deep hunger to pursue God, to know Him more, and to persevere through hard times in the ups and downs of life. He is with me. He shows His love to me in a thousand different ways! I continue my journey of faith and trust. I was baptised by total immersion at Lincoln Free Church not long after I became a Christian. It was in a portable baptistry. You have to climb up stepladders and step down into the pool! I was the last in a queue of 22 people getting baptised that day!

"Repent and be baptised, every one of you, in the Name of Jesus Christ for the forgiveness of your sins. And you will receive the gift of the Holy Spirit. The promise is for you and your children, and for all who are far off, for all whom the Lord our God will call."

Acts 2:38 (NIV).

I received the gift of the Holy Spirit too. That is the baptism of the Spirit. Those wanting to receive this gift stayed after the Sunday evening service. We sat in the back room of the church in a circle. Maybe 12 or so of us. I am hungry to receive whatever God wants to give!

We prayed and asked God to fill us with the Holy Spirit. It is quiet, it is gentle, though it's not the same for everyone! I believe that I received the Spirit. Simple faith! Later that same night, one word kept coming to my mind. It was the beginning of a prayer language called praying in tongues; a beautiful, powerful gift for praying and connecting with God every day. I am strengthened and renewed, set on fire with a passion for God. I feel alive!

READY…GO!

> God wants you to know Him. He wants you to see yourself as He sees you. A world changer, a hero, a champion, and pioneer, called to do exploits.

"The people who know their God shall be strong, and carry out great exploits!"

Daniel 11:32 (NKJV).

Reflect on this verse; consider what exploits God is calling you to do. There is power in your testimony. Write your story here:

_____
_____
_____
_____
_____
_____
_____

READY...GO!

Chapter 3

God's Masterpiece

Snow is fluttering down from the sky. Gentle. Soft. Silent. A pure white blanket covers the landscape. 3 months in Latvia. January, February and March; the coldest winter for 10 years bites my toes! Latvia is a country on the Baltic Sea, nestled between Lithuania and Estonia. I was excited to be there as I met the beautiful Latvian people. My home is a small flat, in a high-rise block in the capital city of Riga.

My host is a lovely Grandmother, and her 4-year-old granddaughter. Amazing hospitality. Soon, I am part of the family. I looked at a book with the little girl. We somehow communicated together, even though I don't speak Russian or Latvian! I was there to share the love of Jesus and encourage different churches. Certainly, this family had seen a great deal of tragedy. A project to help street children is in its early stages. As I walked the streets in the city, I felt God's heart of mercy and compassion. I see intoxicated bodies slumped over piles of snow on the edges of the pavement. High alcohol intake takes its toll and their children suffer.

The Baltic Sea is frozen, 3-feet thick! Fishermen dotted around the vast expanse of ice, drill holes so they can lower their fishing rods into the water below. Just like in a cartoon picture! A fascinating experience to walk on the sea of ice, apart from being chased by some very large birds! A few flakes of snow began to fall from the sky. Tiny flakes landed on my pink padded jacket.

I looked at my arm and on the sleeve of my coat, I saw very tiny 6-sided snowflakes. Amazingly formed! The hexagonal pattern is clearly visible! So beautiful. A kiss from heaven! A miracle and delight to see God's wonderful creation. The temperature is low, minus 22 degrees. There is enough moisture in the atmosphere to create exactly the right conditions for this spectacular show! Each

READY...GO!

snowflake is unique, intricately, and delicately designed, just like you are!

"You formed my innermost being, shaping my delicate inside and my intricate outside, and wove them all together in my mother's womb. I thank You God, for making me so mysteriously complex! Everything You do is marvellously breath-taking. It simply amazes me to think about it! How thoroughly You know me, Lord! You even formed every bone in my body when You created me in the Secret Place, carefully, skilfully shaping me from nothing to something. You saw who You created me to be before I became me! Before I'd ever seen the light of day, the number of days You planned for me were already recorded in Your book."

Psalm 139: 13-16 (TPT).

How awesome that we have always existed within God's heart even before the world came into being! What an amazing God! I hear Father God saying:

"You are designed to bring Me Glory in a way no-one else can. You are created to live here and now in this generation for a purpose. No-one has the same personality and talents as you do to fulfil My plans and purposes. You are irreplaceable. My Son, Jesus, paid the highest price possible by dying on the Cross for you, to bring life, wholeness, forgiveness, healing, deliverance, and restoration."

What a wonderful, gracious, loving, and merciful God! I give Him thanks and praise. He shows us the truth of who we are.

You are an original work of art! You are priceless and valuable.

"And you shall know the truth, and the truth shall make you free."

John 8:32 (NKJV).

READY...GO!

Marvel at God's creation. An intricate snowflake in Latvia; so beautiful! God has made you beautiful, chosen, and not rejected. Speak it out! Write it here:

_____

_____

_____

_____

_____

_____

_____

READY...GO!

Chapter 4

Up, up, and Away!

Waiting for a window of good weather. Excitement and anticipation are building. Will the balloon fly today? A gentle breeze is blowing over the beautiful Yorkshire countryside. Clouds are parting; the sun begins to shine. Perfect! Safety checks are being made. The hot air balloon is a spectacular sight on the ground; bright colours of green, red, yellow, orange, and blue.

Preparations are made for the flight; it is partially inflated with fans, until the burners in the balloon take over. A couple of steps up into the rectangular shape woven wicker basket. The adventure begins with 10 or so fellow passengers. Standing in one of the compartments; I hear the flame jets roar noisily. Our pilot is inflating the balloon and heating up the air. Rope tethers untied. Up, up and away! Exciting!

The wind is master of our travel moving us to an unknown destination. The balloon ascends, as the pilot continues to inject hot air. I feel the heat of the flames. I feel safe. Floating through the air, the burners cease their roar. It is quiet and still. The tranquillity is awe-inspiring; we float high above the ground. A gentle breeze directs our course. We looked down as the balloon drifts across a river. A small dot of our shadow reflects in it! We look across the countryside to see the extravagant beauty of God's creation.

We descended to lower heights along the winding river. Children played on the banks either side. We waved and they waved back as the balloon swooped along. The pilot injected more hot air into the balloon. Once again, we rise up skimming the hedges! Now high in the sky again. Sadly, after an hour or so, it was time to look for somewhere to land. The pilot located a large field; we were then about 5 miles from the launch site. We started to descend as hot air was gradually released.

READY...GO!

He asked us to get into a landing position, bend our knees and hold tight to a leather strap. We landed with a jolt, a little bounce and a skid! We were safe! A group of happy passengers helped to deflate and fold up the balloon. A pick-up truck soon arrived to take us and the balloon back to base. We enjoyed a champagne toast as we clutched our certificate and photograph of the balloon. Evidence of our amazing adventure! What a picture of our walk with God.

Wind is a biblical symbol of the Holy Spirit, and fire too. I heard the Lord saying:

"Just as balloonists rely on the wind, so rely on the wind of the Holy Spirit to lead and guide you in your journey of faith. Fresh surrender. New adventures. Rise up and break free of those things that hold you down and hinder you. Untie the ropes, ready for take-off! Let Me show you what is holding you back. Is it unforgiveness, failure, guilt or shame? Give them to Me. Drop the weights so you can ascend into My Glory cloud. You will soar. I will show you wonderful things as I navigate. Enjoy it! Don't play safe! Be baptised with the Holy Spirit and fire. You will receive power to be My witnesses. I created in you a burning passion that moves you forward, aligning you with My will. The flames will cause others to soar, to go higher in Me. The Holy Spirit sends the fire and the wind. A life of adventure with Me!"

> **The Spirit, like the wind, moves where He wants. Gloriously unpredictable and at times, suddenly!**

"The wind blows where it wishes, and you hear the sound of it, but cannot tell where it comes from and where it goes. So, is everyone who is born of the Spirit."

John 3:8 (NKJV).

READY…GO!

Reflect on and lay down any weights that might be preventing you from take-off. Do you have any 'unexpected' course changes as you think back through your life?

_____

_____

_____

_____

_____

_____

_____

READY…GO!

Chapter 5

Orchestra on the Streets

A melodious sound rings out across the cobbled streets in the city Square of Prague. I was on holiday and ambled along with other tourists. We came across an open-air concert. Musicians were assembled right in the middle of the Square on the cobbles! Strings, woodwind, brass, and percussion instruments tuned up. We felt the vibrations watching each one play in a beautiful symphony. We stopped and listened.

Suddenly, the conductor catches my eye and walks up to me. He gives me his baton indicating for me to conduct! Feeling rather awkward for a few seconds, I embraced the challenge. I did not have any clue on how it was done, apart from a little experience of being part of an orchestra at school! I took the baton and conducted the orchestra! More realistically, I frantically waved my arms around, then took a bow! I contemplated this scenario with the Lord. What is He saying? I heard these words:

"I bring you together in an orchestra to make a beautiful symphony, a harmonious sound for the Father's Will. I communicate timing to you. I lead and teach you as you fix your gaze on Me. Connected one to another, in tune with My heart to display Jesus on the earth. I make sure the volume of the instruments is balanced so no-one is drowned out. Harmony and joy. The world sees and hears My Son, Jesus. Your instrument is vital to the *whole*. Your gifts, your life, and your voice fill the gap. The sound of the melody is magnificent. Others need you as you need them. Be released to find your place. The orchestra is waiting. I am raising up an army to make a missional church; a family, not a programme, but mission at the very core of the Church's purpose for being."

Could the orchestra in the open air be comparable with outreach teams on the streets? Teams who go out to love and serve our

READY…GO!

communities and share the Gospel. The Lord says: "As teams go out I hear a beautiful sound giving Glory to My Name. Use your voice! It is a trumpet sound permeating the sound waves wherever you go to bring healing, deliverance, salvation, and peace. *"Lift up your voice like a trumpet." Isaiah 58:1 (NKJV)*

The trumpet is a battle signal. It is a wake-up call to repentance. Declare freedom! My Word is a two-edge sword; proclaim it boldly. Announce the Good News of the Kingdom. I am Heavens great orchestrator, creating compositions for the Father's Will. Will you be part of My Orchestra? My timing is perfect. I will lead you. I will provide for all you need. You are chosen, appointed and anointed. You are valued and loved. I am calling you to belong."

What a privilege and honour it is to be part of the orchestra! Jesus prays for the unity of all believers who will witness His divine mission. God connects hearts of believers together to display Christ on earth.

"That they all may be one, as You Father, are in Me, and I in You; that they also may be one in us, that the world may believe that You sent Me. And the Glory which You gave Me, I have given them, that they may be one just as We are one."

John 17:21-22 (NKJV).

Let the orchestra begin! Express your thoughts on how you are part of the melody:

_____

_____

_____

_____

_____

_____

_____

READY…GO!

Chapter 6

Playdough!

Rolling, squishing, moulding, breaking, pinching and flattening! Developing muscle strength. Playdough wins the day! Working with children for many years, I have discovered how nearly everyone loves playdough; me included! It develops creativity, builds imagination, vocabulary, literacy and numeracy! Definitely something every parent and children's worker should have in their messy play collection! Endless opportunities for fun. A brilliant accompaniment for storytelling and bringing characters to life with playdough. Children remember!

At the nursery where I work, I tell the story of Jesus' birth at Christmas time as we play with the playdough. We make the stable, animals, angels, stars, Mary and Joseph, shepherds and three kings. We then put the playdough baby Jesus in the manger. Next time, they do all the storytelling! They don't forget it! Making our own playdough is best, especially playing with it while it's still warm, soft, and pliable! We add colour with food colouring, and sometimes glitter, spices or fragrant essences. A great delight!

Clay is not as pliable as playdough, though very similar. I am reminded that we are the clay. I have watched potters at work in Poole Pottery. There is definitely that rolling, squishing, moulding, breaking, pinching, and flattening in the hands of the potter! The wheel is controlled by a foot pedal. The potter uses their hands and some tools to shape the clay by applying pressure. Shaping it as seems best to the potter. Lovingly, patiently.

"But now, O Lord, You are our Father; We are the clay, and You our potter; and all we are the work of Your hand."

Isaiah 64:8 (NKJV).

READY...GO!

I heard the Lord saying:

"I am the Master Potter. As you watch a lump of clay on a Potter's wheel, so I mould and re-shape you in My hands. I am transforming you. I never give up. I know the design. You are unique. I am fashioning you, your character. My plans for you are vast. Yes, there are struggles in the transformation process. Yield to Me; trust Me. Do not fear. It requires a yielding of mindsets, opinions and agendas. I am humbling you. A soft, pliable, and teachable heart in My hands. I am crafting you into a vessel of honour, being conformed to the likeness of My Son. Come to Me as you are. I know what is best for you. I am refining you for the King's service."

What a privilege to be in the King's service! He shapes us *inwardly*, making us fit for His use. He remakes and shapes us as we yield to the Potter. He knows how to work with us. He knows us intimately. Clay pots need to go to the kiln for firing before they become useable. At times, we are placed in that kiln and the fires of life turn us into stronger vessels.

God's Hands reshape our broken dreams. Certainly, the heartache of miscarriage was part of the fire for me. Also, the challenge of being a single parent when my daughter was seven. It catapulted me into the arms of a loving heavenly Father who surrounded me with His love, care, and provision. He wants to mould us and make us more like Him.

"He has made everything beautiful in its time."

Ecclesiastes 3:11 (NKJV).

How wonderful to know the purpose for which we have been uniquely made and chosen. God created man out of the dust of the ground.

READY...GO!

"And the Lord God formed man of the dust of the ground, and breathed into his nostrils the breath of life; and man became a living being."

Genesis 2:7 (NKJV).

The Hebrew word for dust is *'aphar'* – clay is one meaning. So, we who are jars of clay, weak and fragile, can be instruments of the power of God! In our weakness, God fills us and the power of the Holy Spirit works through us as dynamite! The Greek word used for power is *dunamis*; similar to the English word for dynamite. The original meaning is "A power that multiplies itself!"

When God's Spirit links with our prayers, the seed comes to life in us and flows out to others. Pressure against us is often aimed at our purpose and destiny, but your destiny will break open. We can exercise faith in the face of everything that says otherwise; it releases the atmosphere of Heaven.

"But we have this treasure in jars of clay to show that this all-surpassing power is from God and not from us."

2 Corinthians 4:7 (NIV).

Lord, I want a soft, responsive heart to You. Melt me, mould me and fill me. Change my heart.

"I will give you a new heart and put a new spirit in you; I will remove from you your heart of stone, and give you a heart of flesh. And I will put my Spirit in you, and move you to follow my decrees and be careful to keep my laws."

Ezekiel 36:26-27 (NIV).

READY…GO!

"Spirit of the living God; fall afresh on me." Ask Him to fill you. What is God is saying to you? You are clay in the potter's hands. Write your thoughts here:

_____

_____

_____

_____

_____

_____

_____

READY...GO!

Chapter 7

No Microwave Hatchings!

A beautiful lake. Still and calm, glistening in the sun. All around the edges of the lake at ground level, there are many nests that contain eggs. Some eggs are hatching. God is showing me this picture in a dream. He says "I put you in charge of eggs that are delicate and fragile. Each one hatches in My perfect timing."

Birds that nest on the ground such as ducks, geese and swans are very vulnerable to predators. However, they are well camouflaged to blend in with the habitat. I walk around the lake and see many eggs. Some are already hatched; others are there for a long time.

The Lord says: "My plans cannot be rushed – no microwave hatchings! You cannot speed up the process. My timing is perfect for My plans to unfurl in your life, others' lives, and those for whom you pray. Salvation, health, healing and miracles are on their way! Speak My Word; watch and pray. Decree and declare My promises over yourself, your family; whatever is on your heart. It is incubating! Declare protection from predators! The incubation period may seem long, but don't give up. Breakthrough is coming and the wonders of new life shall start to appear."

In the natural, some eggs hatch quickly and others take a long time. The shortest is 9-10 days, while the albatross takes 11 weeks! The Lord says "Although I put you in charge of the eggs, you cannot help with the hatching, because it will cause injury. The chick pecks into the air sac on the side of the inner egg to get more oxygen to breathe. In My time, I breathe new life into My plans and purposes. Be patient. Love. Pray. Protect and guard. I trust you. When the chick is hatched, you can direct it to the water. Nurture new believers and lead them to the pure life-giving waters. Nurture the promises that begin to hatch."

READY...GO!

Waiting is hard, but it teaches us so much! God's promise to Joseph purged his character until it was time for his dreams to come true in reference to Psalm 105:19. He waited over 13 years for the vision God gave him to be realised.

"My times are in Your Hands."

Psalm 31:15 (NKJV).

Waiting strengthens our faith; it teaches us to believe God, even when we can't see the promise.

"Imitate those who through faith and patience inherit what has been promised."

Hebrews 6:12 (NIV).

It is hard when our prayers don't seem to be answered including prayers for ourselves and others. In the waiting season, keep serving, keep trusting and depending on God. He knows best! He delays because He loves and desires to give us something far better than we could ever ask.

"'For My thoughts are not your thoughts, nor are your ways My ways,' says the Lord. 'For as the Heavens are higher than the earth, so My ways are higher than your ways, and My thoughts than your thoughts.'"

Isaiah 55:8-9 (NKJV).

Write what you hear God saying to you. Speak out God's Word and see His promises *hatch* in His perfect timing. Let us continue to fix our eyes on Jesus.

READY…GO!

"Write the vision and make it plain on tablets, that he may run who reads it. For the vision is yet for an appointed time; but at the end, it will speak and it will not lie. Though it tarries, wait for it because it will surely come; it will not tarry."

Habakkuk 2:2-3 (NKJV).

What eggs are you incubating in your life? Ask God if anything is delaying you:

_____

_____

_____

_____

_____

_____

READY...GO!

Chapter 8

First Glimpse of Dawn

I sat on the cold sand on the beach in Caesarea; Israel, in the early hours of the morning! I looked up to see the star-studded sky like twinkling diamonds. Our first destination straight from Tel Aviv airport on a 10-day tour of Israel. It is pitch black. No noise apart from the waves lapping gently on the Mediterranean shore. A time to be still and reflect after a long journey from the UK.

God's Presence is calming, restoring and strengthening. We wait excitedly and expectantly for the first glimpse of dawn. Just before the sun rises, the sky is at its blackest. Little by little, the sky fills with orange, pink and gold colours. The mist lifts. Golden rays are breaking through, giving colour to the clouds; the horizon appears. A beautiful invitation to a new day! The long dark night is over. The world awakes. The birds begin to sing as the sun comes up. An awe-inspiring start in stillness and quiet.

"Be still and know that I am God; I will be exalted among the nations; I will be exalted in the earth!"

Psalm 46:10 (NKJV).

As I reflect on this beautiful beginning to our tour in Israel, I am drawn to consider how important Sabbath rest is at the beginning of our week! A time to set our hearts on Him and rest from our usual work.

"Thus, the heavens and the earth and all the host of them were finished. And on the seventh day, God ended His work which He had done, and He rested on the seventh day from all His work which He had done. Then God blessed the seventh day and sanctified it,

READY...GO!

because in it, He rested from all His work which God had created and made."

Genesis 2:1-3 (NKJV).

God created the Sabbath after He created Adam and Eve. So, their first day was a Sabbath! Marvellous! God made it to bless them for rest and enjoyment! It is not about any rules to keep, but a beautiful invitation to set apart 1 day a week for rest, for physical health and spiritual well-being. Each person's Sabbath will be different. What energises you? Time alone? Being with others? It will also depend on your season of life and your circumstances, but do something you like! Get together with friends; read, make your favourite meal, nap, walk, meditate, pray, listen to music, maybe watch a film. It might be a different day each week; it doesn't have to be a Sunday. The Sabbath is made for our benefit.

"And He said to them, 'The Sabbath was made for man, and not man for the Sabbath. Therefore, the Son of Man is also Lord of the Sabbath.'"

Mark 2:27-28 (NKJV).

Setting aside one day a week is the fourth of the Ten Commandments given to Moses up the mountain, and is actually written by the finger of God on the stone tablets. *"Remember the Sabbath day to keep it Holy."*

Laws in the Old Covenant could not impart life or power to fulfil its demands. Jesus' sacrifice was complete and opened the way for forgiveness and reconciliation. It is a Covenant of promise for those who through faith, accept Jesus and commit themselves to Him. God says He will write His laws on our hearts. We receive a new heart; a heart of flesh instead of a heart of stone. A heart to know Him and to be in His Presence each day.

"For this is the covenant that I will make with the house of Israel after those days, says the Lord; I will put My laws in their mind and

READY...GO!

write them on their hearts, and I will be their God, and they shall be My people."

Hebrews 8:10 (NKJV).

So, with the Sabbath *law,* God has written it on our hearts. We have an inbuilt rhythm to follow a pattern of 6 days' work and 1 days' rest. We can enter into God's rest and then work from that position of rest! The first glimpse of dawn on Caesarea beach in Israel is the reminder of God's creative Sabbath rest. The sun rises, the light comes; a new day begins as we tour the Holy Land. So many memories, especially floating on the Dead Sea! Also, our beautiful experience at the Garden Tomb, most likely the site of Jesus' burial and resurrection. God's peace and Presence were tangible.

"The path of the righteous is like the first gleam of dawn, shining ever brighter till the full light of day."

Proverbs 4:18 (NIV).

Allow God's rhythm to organise your time. Jot down any ideas:

_____
_____
_____
_____
_____
_____
_____

READY...GO!

Chapter 9

Daddy, do you see me?

A little girl with a princess dress on does a twirl for everyone to see! I see this scenario in my work place at nursery! So, too, when little girls do a twirl for their Daddy with their sparkling dress on, they are really asking two questions: "Do you see me?" and "Do you *like* what you see?" These are questions in our own hearts too.

Father God says: "I see you. You are beautiful to Me. You move My heart like nobody else does. You are irreplaceable. I love to speak to you. I am not just tolerating you. You are chosen. I enjoy you and I love to hear your voice. I like what I see!"

Human fathers show you an imperfect representation of what Father God is like; we need to break out of that containment. As a child, my father sometimes said "Children should be seen and not heard!" There were many treasured times to remember, like sitting on his shoulders as a small child, as he showed me all the flowers in the garden! When I was about 7 or 8, I used to sit on the stool next to him as he played the church organ on a Saturday morning! It was a special time. The human heart is created with a longing for the assurance that we are enjoyed by the Father.

"How great is the love the Father has lavished on us, that we should be called children of God! And that is what we are!"

1 John 3:1 (NIV).

God wants a heart-relationship with us, not obedience to a set of rules. Forgiving isn't just something He does; it is His very nature to be merciful; a God who pardons. As we ask Him to forgive us of our sins and invite Jesus into our lives, God becomes our Father in

READY…GO!

Heaven. Forgiveness and repentance opens our hearts. We receive adoption as sons, in reference to Galatians 4:5. God's love for us is unconditional. God loves to heal broken hearts. He has not abandoned us. He suffered all that we have gone through and more.

There is healing for the guilt of our selfishness, and the consequences of it; the scars and wounds we bear in our personalities. It is freeing to let go, to let God heal our lives. Emotional healing is a process and God wants to bring us into maturity as His sons to build character. Our life is revolutionised as we see how the Father feels about us.

We can acknowledge our need of healing as we are honest with ourselves. Tell God your hurts, fears and disappointments. Unless you accept responsibility for your actions, your healing is blocked. Receive His grace, love, acceptance and forgiveness. You are secure in Him and can trust God and others. We are not created to be prisoners of our emotions.

We do need to forgive those who have hurt us; however, it isn't easy. It's tough, but peace and freedom are what we gain. It is not forgetting a wrong, but releasing them into God's Hands, and letting go of past hurts. When we hold onto anger, resentment, and other negative emotions towards others, it can lead to stress and anxiety and even physical health problems. God wants you to know the peace of His forgiveness as you forgive others. Ask Him to help you forgive.

> **Jesus lived out of connectedness to the Father. We have that privilege too!**

"The Son can do nothing by Himself; He can do only what He sees His Father doing, because whatever the Father does, the Son also does."

John 5:19 (NIV).

READY…GO!

"Anyone who has seen me has seen the Father."

John 14:9 (NKJV).

The Father loves us the same way He loves Jesus. How wonderful is that truth! The Blood of Jesus reconnects us to the Father. You are chosen; you are wanted and you bring Father God pleasure. He enjoys you! The first time I remember God speaking to me as Father was in the early days of my career. I began to feel teaching wasn't something I wanted to do for the rest of my life. I heard the loving voice of my Father God. Somehow, I instinctively knew it was Father speaking! He said "What would you *like* to do?" I realised at this point He wasn't controlling and demanding, but intimate and involved. He was giving me a choice.

What a loving and gracious Father! My choice was wanting to work with *nursery* age children. Since then, my work has included nannying and childminding, and setting up and managing a Day Nursery; I called it Acorn Nursery. God was speaking to me then about seeds!

Having my own daughter is precious! Lots of fun! Also, many opportunities to share the Good News of the Gospel leading children's clubs in church, at Rhyme Time and Messy Church. I also worked as a Playleader for Home Start and volunteered to support families in their homes. God is asking the question to you: "What would *you* like to do?"

Orphans live in their own strength, but thank God that we are no longer orphans! As we release the spirit of adoption, Father God gives us identity as a son; we can never earn it. Receive it. He is waiting for you with arms open wide! He is the Father you've always longed for.

"Because you are sons, God sent the Spirit of His Son into our hearts; the Spirit who calls out, Abba Father. So, you are no longer

READY…GO!

a slave but a son, and since you are a son, God has made you also an heir."

Galatians 4:6-7 (NIV).

Thank you, Father that Your thoughts towards me outnumber the grains of sand on the seashore. Write your thoughts towards Father God below:

_____

_____

_____

_____

_____

_____

_____

READY…GO!

Chapter 10

At the Woollen Mill

The shuttles on the loom were flying at great speed. The sheep sheared, the wool cleaned and carded. Yarn is spun and dyed, and either woven or knitted. A lengthy process at the Welsh Woollen Mill! An amazing multi-step process. Machinery makes it a faster process today than in times gone by.

The process of transforming a sheep's fleece into soft and cosy wool is truly an art form that needs careful management. It is time consuming, but the end-product has great quality and value. Pure natural wool with no blends or compromises. Different processes in the spinning stages create different kinds of yarn for distinct final products. Tweeds, flannel, blankets, carpets and wool for knitting or tapestry. It was captivating watching the looms on which the fabrics were woven. Beautiful patterns started to emerge. Nothing was wasted. Offcuts were sold to crafters!

There is a saying that goes: 'I have been through the mill' and I began to understand the deeper meaning after visiting the woollen mill! Wonderful creations came out of the woollen mill, but one thing is sure; the process is long! God has a plan and we can trust His workings and timings in making all things beautiful. He knows the end from the beginning!

The Master Weaver is making you strong. He lovingly crafts your life. He weaves in His love, vision, gifts and flexibility. Some fabrics are designed to stretch and expand to make room for growth. Maternity clothes!

We need to be flexible enough to make room for the birth of God's Promises. Trust in His Process. He knows. He cares!

READY...GO!

This poem I wrote called "He Knows, He Cares" captivates God's heart of compassion for us.

The Lord delights in His chosen ones,
He sees our every desire,
He leads us by the flowing streams
And forever leads us higher.

Though at times we cannot see,
The way ahead seems dim,
We can trust the living Lord
And cast our cares on Him.

I know your ways, your thoughts, your life,
Know My cleansing within,
I have made you a son of God,
A priest and a King.

Walk in the light and praise your God,
Rest secure in Me,
My arms surround you, lift you up,
The way of the Kingdom you'll see.

Fix your eyes on Me alone,
Do not despair of life,
See how I love you, have paid the price,
Redeemed, set free from strife.

Set your heart on things above,
Move in possess the land,
Get lost in wonder, love and praise,
In royal robes we stand.

On the looms at the woollen mill, the fabrics were hidden while being woven; yet, there is excitement and anticipation for what will emerge! I recall the unknown years of Jesus' life, referring to the period between His childhood and the beginning of His ministry. They are not recorded in the New Testament, sometimes called the *hidden years*. They were very significant years in which Jesus *"grew*

READY...GO!

in wisdom and stature and in favour with God and men" in reference to Luke 2:52 (NIV).

So, with us, the Master Weaver is making us strong as He weaves *fabric* to contain and carry the work and blessing of God in our lives. He takes pride in us. He loves and enjoys us. Intimacy between the Weaver and the wool. Sometimes, we feel hidden, but God is at work. Thankfully, He knows best! Hearts are woven together for the world to see and touch. We stand in royal robes.

Reflect on what God is weaving into your life. How is He weaving you together with others?

_____

_____

_____

_____

_____

_____

_____

READY…GO!

Chapter 11

Mountain Adventure

The mountains beckon. Rugged, beautiful, majestic and breath-taking! The sun is warming the air in early summer in Austria. Great anticipation and excitement on my third visit! Fresh mountain air, stunning panoramic views. Silence, away from a noisy and busy world. The occasional sound of cow bells clanging and jangling around the necks of roaming cows and goats. Music to my ears! Many walkers explored the mountain along with experienced hikers and mountain bikers. Yodellers too! Cable cars for a quick ascent and descent. A few snow-capped peaks remain. Lush green valleys below. It is invigorating and soul-awakening.

A gondola takes us to the Alpine flower garden on the summit. Spectacular! We took time to stop and admire the amazing views. We purchased a summer card pass for unlimited use on the cable cars and gondolas. We made sure to make the most use of them! My daughter, 13 years old at the time, and I spent our last morning in Austria going up and down the mountain near our hotel in the cable car. We went round the circuit 4 times without getting off enjoying the ride! Our final day in the mountains, admiring the fabulous views; until next time!

I hear the Lord saying: "I am training you, though you have not seen it as training. I am moving in your life in the various circumstances you find yourself in. In the difficulties, you must run to Me. I am strengthening you, equipping you and getting you ready for this season. You will run up and down mountains. You will come to the high places and meet with Me, but you will also go to the valleys to meet people in their brokenness and pain. You will bring them up the mountain. Come to the Secret Place. Spend time with Me up the mountain. I will give you all you need. My provision and affirmation. Then, go to the valleys."

READY…GO!

Jesus often withdrew up to the mountain to spend time with His Father. Mountains were a significant part of His life here on earth; solitary places where He spent time praying, receiving strength and guidance. Mountains are places of healing, revelation and also commissioning. What does it mean for us to spend time up the mountain? Probably not a literal mountain, though what better place than to breathe deeply and commune with the Father! It is an intentional time to be alone with ourselves and with God.

We can tune out the noise and shut down the mental clutter as we listen to His voice. If Jesus shows the need for sustained prayer, then surely, we must follow His example! I have grown to delight in spending time with Him through listening, communing, praying and worshipping; experiencing the thrilling joy of knowing Jesus. It roots me deeply into His love, knowing who He is and the truth of who I am.

"Now, in the morning, having risen a long while before daylight, He went out and departed to a solitary place; and there, He prayed."

Mark 1:35 (NKJV).

Jesus spent time with His Father early in the morning after a busy previous day, healing the sick and casting out demons. As Jesus needed that refreshing to refocus, so do we. Spend time in His Presence and enjoy His embrace. Jesus also spent time praying up the mountain before making important decisions such as choosing His 12 disciples.

"Now, it came to pass in those days that He went out to the mountain to pray, and continued all night in prayer to God. And when it was day, He called His disciples to Himself, and from them, He chose 12 whom He also named Apostles."

Luke 6:12-13 (NKJV).

READY...GO!

> **What works well for you in pursuing God in solitude will depend on your personality and season of life.**

It is not about duty or performance, but an invitation to spend time with Him. Let it become part of your daily rhythm of prayer. Whether you spend 10 minutes, hours, or more, you will be strengthened and renewed. Be persistent. Your prayers are being answered. Give Him thanks and praise in advance.

"But those who wait on the Lord shall renew their strength; they shall mount up with wings like eagles, they shall run and not be weary, they shall walk and not faint."

Isaiah 40:31 (NKJV).

I heard the Lord say:

"Now, it's time to go to the valleys! I am calling you to bring people up the mountain to meet with Me. Those in darkness and despair, defeat and discouragement. Take them by the hand and lead them into My Presence. They will find healing, hope, joy and strength in Me."

As we spend time in God's Presence, we carry a beautiful aroma of His Presence to those around us.

"Now, thanks be to God who always leads us in triumph in Christ, and through us diffuses the fragrance of His knowledge in every place. For we are to God the fragrance of Christ among those who are being saved and among those who are perishing."

2 Corinthians 2:14-15 (NKJV).

READY...GO!

How does spending time in God's Presence strengthen your walk with Him and enable you to reach out to others? Write your answer below:

_____

_____

_____

_____

_____

_____

_____

Chapter 12

A Beached Whale

It is a sad and heart-breaking sight. A whale washed up on a beach. A tragic scene, a struggle for life. The whale desperately tries to swim in the shallows, but the weight only makes it dig deeper into the sands.

Whales are unique, beautiful and graceful creatures. They form friendships, grieve, play, sing and co-operate with one another. Watching whales gliding along in the open sea with sun sparkling on their backs is an awesome sight. Blows of mist spurting in the air. Sea creatures do not want to be stranded on the beach. The ocean is calling; that is where they belong.

Feeling overwhelmed by circumstances and storms of life, I began to feel like a beached whale. Stuck. Impossible situations looming. I felt helpless and hopeless. God's immense love drew me close. A friend invited me to a Mission 24 Conference. The worship was vibrant and passionate with much faith and prayer. God's Presence is real. Believers are on fire for the Lord. A life-changing encounter full of love and power. I found myself swimming again in that vast ocean. Restoration, hope and vision came flooding in. No longer beached, but entering into God's plans and purposes for my life.

I heard the Lord say: "Swim with ease, glide fast and smooth, even though the waters may be turbulent. I have shaped you for this! There are treasures in the deep."

My heart was stirred and was very thankful. I began the Mission24 Impact Training Course online. Much treasure and the truth of God's Word changed me forever. Mission24 is an inter-denominational, Christian movement committed to proclaiming the Good News of Jesus, equipping believers in the Power of the Holy Spirit and making Disciples of all nations.

READY...GO!

The same year, I enrolled on the Mission24 internship in 2019 - 2020, which is now called School of Ministry and Mission: "A year to transform your life!" and so it did! Within the first two weeks, I led my Mum to the Lord as she prayed the Salvation prayer giving her life to God. Another chapter on that! We covered many subjects in monthly lectures such as discipleship, the believer's authority, faith, covenant, ministering healing, moving in the prophetic, deliverance, the Father heart of God, revival history, books to read, essays to write, bible studies and opportunities for mission. In a nutshell, it was a breath of fresh air!

In the analogy of the beached whale, I find it is an ocean of God's love and mercy. God wants us to be part of His plan to GO into all the world. My first mission was in Derby. It was wonderful seeing other people's lives transformed and changed. By the end of the mission, I felt my life being more impacted than theirs! Never did I imagine I'd be on the streets sharing the Gospel! God has His Ways! On missions, or with a local team in my home town, we see God touching hearts, people giving their lives to God and divine healings. God tells us to heal the sick. He works through us as we lay hands on sick people.

"They will place their hands on sick people and they will get well."

Mark 16:18 (NIV).

One day, we stopped to talk to an Albanian lady. She immediately rang her Mum in Albania, and asked us to pray for her mum on the phone for a particular need, her daughter translating! We didn't have to go far that day to take the Gospel to the nations!

Often, it takes hard and desperate times to propel us into God's best purposes. How have you found this to be true?

READY...GO!

READY…GO!

Chapter 13

All Change!

A train journey is always an exciting adventure. I stepped onto the Underground, a rail network across the city of London, the Tube. I have a connecting train to catch from one mainline station to another. My destination; the South Coast to visit family. It is buzzing with activity. Lots of hustle and bustle! Passengers are rushing, searching for their trains, or looking for railway workers for assistance!

Whistles blowing; there was lots of noise as I reached my platform. I saw the train coming through the tunnel. I felt the rumbling and vibrations as the train screeched to a halt. Then, the familiar announcement: "Doors are opening; please mind the gap!" I got on the train with my suitcase and sat down. The doors closed; we started to gain speed. A few stations later, the train came to an abrupt stop.

A loud speaker announces: "This train has reached its destination. All change!" This takes me by surprise. We have clearly not reached our intended destination! The words "All Change" seem to hang in the air. I needed to find a different route to the mainline station for the next part of my journey. I continued and wondered what God was showing me at that time?

I hear the Lord saying, "Yes! All Change! I am making changes. Sometimes, changes are sudden and unexpected, but trust Me. I am making a way where there is no way. We are going on adventures together. I am faithful and all powerful. A season of transition and change. Yes, I am changing *you* and transforming you into a different person! It is time to lay some things down and give a fresh *yes* to others."

Time to bury the Acorn! As Manager of the Acorn Nursery for 6 years, it was the greatest joy to look after the little 'acorns!' We had children ages between 6 weeks old and 4 years old. A wonderful

READY...GO!

privilege to work with them with an amazing team of staff. It is good to remember what God did in the past and be thankful, but always respond to God's call to move on and follow His Spirit. Sometimes, we sang a little song at nursery:

I love the sun; it shines on me,
God made the sun and God made me! (Rain and wind verses too!).

One little boy went home singing this song to his Mum. She invited me to her house to explain why we were singing it, and said that we should be teaching from a scientific point of view! I listened to her concerns, then highlighted the Gospel story. Some years later, I found out she became a Christian! Seeds were sown and a harvest reaped! Seed, 'time,' and harvest!

> **Don't be discouraged; it often takes time for the harvest to come!**

God speaks to us most often in a loud thought! I hear Him say: "Lay down your business to be about My Father's business." I prayed and asked God for clarity. I sensed that He was asking me to pass the baton to one of my colleagues that was keen to take on the business. I knew the nursery wasn't my lane to run in anymore. Neither do I know what is next, but I took a leap of faith! God is faithful and I trust Him to catch me just as a little child jumps into the arms of the Father. The child has no doubt that his dad will catch him!

Transitions and changes are not easy. A time to stay close to God more than ever before. These times can be confusing and overwhelming. Anointings change and we change. A closed door inevitably means a new one is opening, when the time is ready. It is through times of change and transition that God uses to transform us into His likeness. He draws us close and reminds us that our lives belong to Him. He knows best; we do not need to worry about what tomorrow will bring. We can have that childlike trust.

READY...GO!

"He called a little child and had him stand among them. And He said: "I tell you the truth, unless you change and become like little children, you will never enter the kingdom of heaven."

Matthew 18:2-3 (NIV).

Just as little children don't worry where food, shelter and comfort are going to come from, we can absolutely depend on our Father God in these times, and trust that He will provide all we need! Even though we don't see what is next, we can step out just as Abraham did, in faith! He was called by God to leave his own country and people, to journey to a new land that God had promised, and that His "seed" would inherit the land.

"By faith, Abraham obeyed when he was called to go out to the place which he would receive as an inheritance. And he went out, not knowing where he was going."

Hebrews 11:8 (NKJV).

Is God asking you to give a fresh yes to anything?

_____
_____
_____
_____
_____
_____
_____

READY...GO!

Chapter 14

Crown Jewels

Ready for a trip to the Jewel House in the Tower of London to see the Crown Jewels with my grandparents in summer around the mid-60s. My favourite time as a child; two weeks with my Gran and Grandad! They lived a train ride away from London. We arrived at the tower to see a myriad of glistening jewels shining brightly, reflecting light. Gold, rubies, amethysts, diamonds, sapphires, garnet, topazes, emeralds and pearls!

The Crown Jewels are the nation's most precious treasure; more than a hundred objects, and over 23 thousand gemstones! We saw Coronation Regalia, crowns, sceptres, orbs, swords and rings worn by Sovereigns. They were kept in the Jewel House, and represent over 8 hundred years of the history of British Monarchy. It was awe inspiring, imagining the value and worth of each one! I'm not one for wearing much jewellery, but the beauty of these jewels encrusted in the crowns caught my attention! They were stunning. I think of these Bible verses of how God crowns us:

"Praise the Lord, O my soul; and forget not all His benefits, who forgives all your sins, and heals all your diseases, who redeems your life from the pit, and crowns you with love and compassion, who satisfies your desires with good things, so that your youth is renewed like the eagles."

Psalm 103:2-4 (NIV).

God's kindness and love are a crown on our heads. God rescues us from the pit, forgives us, heals us and abundantly restores us. He crowns us with His love and compassion. A great exchange! He delights in us. We have a crown to wear and we need to keep our heads held high!

READY...GO!

"For the Lord takes delight in His people; He crowns the humble with Salvation."

Psalm 149:4 (NIV).

So, what do crowns represent biblically? They represent the authority every believer is called to walk in. They symbolise royalty. We are royal!

"To Him who loved us and washed us from our sins in His own blood, and has made us kings and priests to His God and Father; to Him be Glory and dominion forever and ever. Amen."

Revelation 1:5-6 (NKJV).

Jesus loves us and washes us from our sins by His Blood. Roman soldiers pressed a crown of thorns into His head at the crucifixion; and He endured indescribable pain on our behalf for our sin, as He hung on the cross. He was humiliated and mocked for His claims of being King. The crown actually demonstrates who He is. It is a symbol of the curse in reference to Genesis 3:18 – the thorns and thistles in the garden of Eden. He is the One who breaks the curse of sin. His death paved the way for the glorious resurrection; the crown of thorns became a crown of life! Hallelujah! Jesus heals today. The crown of thorns was worn by our Lord so that we could have sound minds, physical healing and new life in abundance. He redeems us!

We are now kings and priests to advance God's Kingdom. We represent the King of Kings! A policeman with his uniform on can stop or direct traffic because of who he is, and who he represents. We have delegated authority to bring in His rule by prayer warfare, proclaiming the Gospel and expecting the miraculous works of God. As we worship before God's throne, we prepare a place for God among us. We welcome Him:

READY…GO!

"You are Holy, enthroned in the praises of Israel."

Psalm 22:3 (NKJV).

Worship is key to entering into His presence and meeting with God. He is with us; often in healings, miracles, conviction of sin, prophecy and salvation. There are crowns waiting for you to finish the race! We are saved by faith alone, not by works, but our works will be rewarded in heaven on the completion of our earthly salvation experience. We will cast our crowns at His feet to honour Him and lay them down as a tribute to the One who created us, saved us, gifted us, equipped us and currently lives in us! There are several specific crowns mentioned in the Bible as follows:

"Finally, there is laid up for me the crown of righteousness which the Lord, the righteous Judge, will give to me on that Day, and not to me only, but also to all who have loved His appearing."

2 Timothy 4:8 (NKJV).

There is a crown of glory that rewards giving, serving and blessing God's flock.

"When the Chief Shepherd appears, you will receive the crown of glory that does not fade away."

1 Peter 5:4 (NKJV).

The crown of rejoicing rewards faithful witnesses to God's Grace.

"For what is our hope, or joy or crown of rejoicing? Is it not even you in the Presence of our Lord Jesus Christ at His coming? For you are our glory and joy."

1 Thessalonians 2:19-20 (NKJV).

READY...GO!

There is an imperishable crown as we run the race with perseverance and diligence.

"Run in such a way as to get the prize. Everyone who competes in the games goes into strict training. They do it to get a crown that will not last; but we do it to get a crown that will last forever."

1 Corinthians 9:24-25 (NIV).

There is the crown of life as we remain steadfast, even to the point of death.

"Blessed is the man who perseveres under trial, because when he has stood the test, he will receive the crown of life that God has promised to those who love him."

James 1:12 (NIV).

"Be faithful, even to the point of death, and I will give you the crown of life."

Revelation 2:10 (NIV).

We can walk now with our heads held high, wearing our crowns! Crowns await us when the race is done. We will cast our crowns at the feet of Jesus and reflect back the glory of Christ, the One who works through us!

You are a precious jewel in God's crown. How does that impact your walk with Him today?

READY...GO!

READY...GO!

Chapter 15

Highway Maintenance

Driving my car one day, I found myself behind a works van. It boldly displayed large black letters on luminous green and red chevrons saying: HIGHWAY MAINTENANCE. It caught my attention! I know God is speaking; the words lingered in my thoughts. Highway maintenance technicians are responsible for providing safety and working order to all highways and roads. They make repairs, road markings and potential hazards safe, and much more! What is God showing me?

"A voice of one calling: "In the desert, prepare the way for the Lord; make straight in the wilderness a highway for our God."

Isaiah 40:3 (NIV).

God wants a highway to our hearts. Am I maintaining the highway in my life for God to come? Am I preparing the way of making straight paths? To know Him and grow into oneness with Him and make Him known? What does it mean practically? How can I do some highway maintenance today to keep the road clear? He highlights 5 areas:

- Full surrender is first. Making repentance part of my life; that is, turning away from sin and running to Christ.

- Secondly; I need to renew my mind by meditating on the Word of God. Just like sheep and cows chew the cud, so meditation is chewing on the word! Read it, repeat it, read it again, speak it, pray it and believe God's Promises for you.

- Thirdly; worship and praise, be obedient and give thanks.

READY…GO!

- Fourth; meeting with other believers.

- Fifth; reaching out to serve others in sharing the Gospel.

There may be roadblocks along the way. Unforgiveness, unconfessed sin and offence can cause roadblocks. Recently, I was driving my car from the Midlands to the South Coast in the UK. Partway on the journey, I encountered a roadblock on one of the major roads. Diversion signs sent me off on a detour through the city of Oxford! Despite me having my Sat Nav and a roadmap set up, I was totally lost!

At one point, I had a strange thought; maybe God's prompting that the car in front knew where to go and I should follow it! It led me to the railway station; a dead end! However, I saw some taxis waiting to go out, a few drivers chatting together outside. I stopped to ask them for directions to get back onto the highway. Just as I drove off, they said "Wait a minute! Follow this taxi; it's going your way!" Thank you, God! He provided the answer through other people, returning me back to the right road.

> **Sometimes in life, we need to ask for help and let others show us the way.**

At times, Godly counsel is the way forward. Likewise; we have the privilege of being a signpost for others. Our God given influence is greater than we know as we point people to Jesus.

"Jesus said, "I am the way, the truth, and the life. No one comes to the Father except through Me."

John 14:6 (NKJV).

READY...GO!

We can build highways in prayer and intercession for those who don't yet know God; to remove the stones and obstacles. There are only two roads. One to eternal separation from God. The other is the road to heaven and eternal life as we come to Jesus through the blood He shed for us on the cross. Much prayer, power and blessing as we intercede to *pull* lives from the Kingdom of darkness.

"Go through! Go through the gates! Prepare the way for the people; build up, build up the highway! Take out the stones, lift up a banner for the peoples!"

Isaiah 62:10 (NKJV).

We can make it a daily choice in our walk with Christ to keep the highway maintained.

"A highway shall be there, and a road, and it shall be called the Highway of Holiness."

Isaiah 35:8 (NKJV).

God is always reaching out to us to bring us close to Himself; to heal, cleanse, forgive and restore. He is calling today. Will you come on God's highway of holiness? There is complete safety, restoration and joy!

"This is what the Lord says: "Stand at the crossroads and look; ask for the ancient paths; ask where the good way is and walk in it, and you will find rest for your souls."

Jeremiah 6:16 (NIV).

READY...GO!

Is God highlighting any Highway Maintenance in your life today?

_____
_____
_____
_____
_____
_____
_____

Chapter 16

Tagged for Blessing!

Spring is on its way! Colours, shapes, sounds and smells; new life all around! Buds bursting into blooms, longer daylight hours, new beginnings and transformations. A peaceful scene of grazing sheep in the field. Lambs are exploring and playing in the sunshine, leaping and bleating.

All sheep are tagged! There is something about sheep I admire! You would see if you came to my house as I have mugs with sheep on, drinks mats, cushions, pictures of sheep and more! Best of all, I know Jesus as my Good Shepherd:

"I am the good shepherd. I know my sheep and my sheep know me, just as the Father knows me and I know the Father, and I lay down my life for the sheep."

John 10:14 (NIV).

My attention is drawn to the ear tags on the sheep. Each individual sheep can be identified and traced! I hear these words of reassurance from the Good Shepherd:

"Your life is marked and ear-tagged. I see you, and have mighty plans for you. I chose you; you are not forgotten. You have purpose in Me. Rest. My love is all you need. Let it reach down into the crevices, those hard-to-reach parts. My heart is overwhelmed when I see you. I love to see you trusting in Me and your devotion to Me. I know your needs and I will provide for you. I see your wonderings about the future, but know that you are marked for fulfilment and abundance. You are tagged for blessing. My Promises for you are Yes and Amen in Christ. I bless you. Know My Spirit on you, in you, and all around you, melting hearts and winning souls, bringing

READY...GO!

lambs into My Kingdom. I lead and protect you. I tend to your wounds and heal you. Let us walk together. Your destiny awaits."

Jesus knows us intimately; we can hear His voice:

"We have the mind of Christ."

1 Corinthians 2:16 (NKJV).

He enjoys us. Let Him speak to you as you position yourself to hear:

"My sheep hear My voice, and I know them, and they follow Me."

John 10:27 (NKJV).

You are *tagged* for blessing. You are already blessed:

"Blessed be the God and Father of our Lord Jesus Christ, who has blessed us with every spiritual blessing in the heavenly places in Christ."

Ephesians 1:3 (NKJV).

God has *already* blessed us with every spiritual blessing! We can walk in that blessing which is truth. Speak it out and declare it. Refuse the lies of the enemy who only comes to steal, kill and destroy.

There are some beautiful promises in Deuteronomy 28 about blessings for obedience. In verses 3-8 (NIV) it reads: *"You will be blessed in the city and blessed in the country. The fruit of your womb will be blessed, and the crops of your land and the young of your livestock – the calves of your herds and the lambs of your flocks.*

READY...GO!

Your basket and your kneading trough will be blessed. You will be blessed when you come in and blessed when you go out. The Lord will grant that the enemies who rise up against you will be defeated before you. They will come at you from one direction but flee from you in seven. The Lord will send a blessing on your barns and on everything you put your hand to. The Lord your God will bless you in the land He is giving you."

Blessings abound! What are your thoughts on being tagged for blessing?'

_____

_____

_____

_____

_____

_____

_____

READY...GO!

Chapter 17

Preparation is Key

I sat in the armchair on a cold November evening at my Father's home. He went to bed; all was quiet. I looked at the logs beside the fireplace I'd brought in earlier from the outhouse. My plan was to light a fire in the open fireplace. I've not lit one before! Logs, kindling, matches and newspaper that I rolled into squills.

As a child, I remember watching my Gran rolling up sheets of newspaper. She tied them round in a loose knot. This is a squill! I was thinking that lighting a fire is easy. I put the logs, kindling and squills in the grate. I lit a match and put it on the kindling. It quickly fizzled out! I tried again and again! Feeling somewhat disappointed, I left it that night with the intention of trying again the next day. I looked on the internet and typed: "How to light a fire!" It was not as easy as I thought it would be. I quickly realised that it said "preparation is key."

There is a technique to laying a fire and building the right structure. I arranged the logs in a square with kindling and squills in the middle, then a couple more logs on top, leaving room for the air to circulate. I was feeling hopeful and prepared. Early next morning, I put a lighted match to the logs and very soon, there was a roaring, blazing fire. Orange flames flickering and dancing with an occasional sizzle, crackle and pop! Warm and cosy. Soon, the beautiful aroma of an open fire fills the room. It was long lasting! I added more logs to keep it burning bright.

Preparation is key. I know God is catching my attention. While on teaching practice at college, my tutor highlighted several times, "good organisational skills" on my reports! Of course, primary school teaching inevitably meant lots of planning and lists. However, it is not so much planning God requires as preparation of the heart.

READY...GO!

> **Sometimes, we cannot control much of what happens in life. What we can do is pray, yield our hearts and lives to God and let Him lead.**

"A man's heart plans his way, but the Lord directs his steps."

Proverbs 16:9 (NKJV).

Jesus prepared for 30 years, for three and a half years of significant ministry. His preparation at home with His parents was important. He learned to work beside Joseph, and like all Jewish boys, he studied the scriptures and Jewish laws.

"And the child grew and became strong in spirit, filled with wisdom; and the grace of God was upon Him."

Luke 2:40 (NKJV).

God is all about preparation for ourselves, but also for those around us, our families, communities and nations! Preparation leads to readiness. God is preparing us for the future, for what He is calling us to do. He is working flexibility in my life, particularly since giving up part-time work in a nursery school recently, to spend more time with my elderly Father; a 5 hour drive away! That too gives me lots of time to write, and to be on the streets most weeks with a local team sharing the Gospel!

John the Baptist prepares the way of the Lord Jesus Christ:

"The voice of one crying in the wilderness: prepare the way of the Lord; make His paths straight."

Luke 3:4 (NKJV).

READY...GO!

Part of Jesus' preparation was His baptism, the Spirit coming upon Him and God's affirmation of Him. It was His commissioning for ministry.

"When He had been baptised, Jesus came up immediately from the water; and behold, the heavens were opened to Him, and He saw the Spirit of God descending like a dove and alighting upon Him. And suddenly, a voice came from heaven saying, 'This is my beloved Son, in whom I am well pleased.'"

Matthew 3:16-17 (NKJV).

After Jesus was baptised, He was led by the Spirit into the wilderness where He fasted and prayed for a 40-day period. Prayer and fasting are always key for preparation. There are many examples in the Bible of God preparing people for significant works. God gave Noah detailed instructions to build an ark for himself and his wife, his three sons and their wives, and for two of each kind of living creatures, in preparation for the flood. Floods destroyed the earth, but Noah and his family were kept safe. God repeats His blessing and promises to Noah *"Be fruitful and multiply, and fill the earth." Genesis 9:1 (NKJV)*

Preparation is an act of faith that God will do what He says. It involves coming to Him and seeking Him with all our hearts, allowing Him to melt and mould us. Be ready and prepared to share the Gospel:

"Preach the word! Be ready in season and out of season."

2 Timothy 4:2 (NKJV).

Finally, preparing for eternal life in God's Kingdom is the *most important* preparation here and now. By faith in Jesus and trusting Him, you can enter into a personal, relationship with God and walk

READY...GO!

into eternity with Him. Give Him a wholehearted "yes" today. He loves you!

"For God so loved the world that He gave His one and only Son, that whoever believes in Him shall not perish, but have eternal life."

John 3:16 (NIV).

It may be that part of God's preparation for you is going on a Training Course for ministry. God knows best how to prepare us!

"The plans of the diligent lead surely to plenty."

Proverbs 21:5 (NKJV).

How is God preparing you?

_____
_____
_____
_____
_____
_____
_____

READY...GO!

Chapter 18

Amazing Grace

It's Easter Day! I reflect on all Jesus has done for me, the wonders of His love and mercy, with gratitude and thankfulness. He died for me to pay the price for my sins. 3 days later, He rose again. He ascended to Heaven, sitting at the right hand of the Father. The Holy Spirit lives in me and I thank Him for the wonderful gift of salvation.

I began to write a poem about my love response to Jesus, and consider afresh His amazing Grace. I hear His loving voice calling me. He says "I call you again to rise up. To know the truth of who I am, and who you are in me. I love you and accept you. I transform you from the inside out. I free you to become all I am calling you to be. My grace empowers you. There are no failures in My Kingdom; My generous grace is enough."

"He will overwhelm your failures with His generous grace. Just make sure you ask, empowered by confident faith without doubting that you will receive."

James 1:5-6 (TPT).

"My grace is sufficient for you, for My strength is made perfect in weakness."

2 Corinthians 12:9 (NKJV).

At the foot of the cross, You see me there,
Waiting, believing, my time will come,
"Yes" He said, "All things are possible!"
I kneel, and rejoice, the Risen Son.

READY...GO!

"Why are you still waiting, kneeling at the cross?
I am not here, but risen indeed,
I come to you now, hold out your hands,
Time to rise, stand, walk, run; your destiny awaits!
Take My hand, keep in step, all will be well,
Time to move on, awakening comes,
Spring shoots reaching through,
Blossoming, flourishing, all is well, and all will be well."
Quickly now, here and there, colours, textures, fragrance fill the air,
Beautiful, my Saviour's plans, He thought of me as He was hanging there.
It shall be all things new, created creature of the Most High God,
Amazing plans, AMAZING GRACE!

What is Grace? It is undeserved favour and blessing; a free gift! It cannot be earned; it is something freely given. Grace is part of God's character. Grace is power for living to do what He wants us to do. That takes the weight off and sets us free to soar in Him!

"And God is able to make all grace abound to you, so that in all things, at all times, having all that you need, you will abound in every good work."

2 Corinthians 9:8 (NIV).

We can come boldly to the throne of grace with our prayers. God's love, help, mercy, forgiveness, power, spiritual gifts, anything we need flows from His throne. A gracious and loving God.

"Let us therefore come boldly to the throne of grace, that we may obtain mercy and find grace to help in time of need."

Hebrews 4:16 (NKJV).

Grace transforms us so that we become more Christ like in how we act, think and speak. Grace propels us to speak to people we wouldn't normally speak to. Transformation happens when we are

READY…GO!

close to Jesus. It is only in His Presence, that we learn 'the unforced rhythms of grace.'

"Are you tired? Worn out? Burned out on religion? Come to Me. Get away with Me, and you'll recover your life. I'll show you how to take a real rest. Walk with me and work with me, watch how I do it. Learn the unforced rhythms of grace. I won't lay anything heavy or ill-fitting on you. Keep company with me and you'll learn to live freely and lightly."

Matthew 11:28-30 (MSG).

How are you discovering the wonders of God's amazing grace?

_____

_____

_____

_____

_____

_____

_____

Chapter 19

Loss and Gain

I knocked on the door of Amelia's little bungalow. She lived on her own. She opened the door. It was my first visit. A couple of other students from the Christian Union at college introduced me to this lovely lady. A lady in her seventies totally blind for a long time. She had glass eyes. She pushed a trolley to guide her, to remain steady. Her long white hair neatly combed and tied back. It shined brightly in the sun; she sat in her armchair by the window.

A radiant face, smooth skin and a beautiful smile. Always a cheerful disposition. She loved talking about Jesus. She had a deep faith in God. I read a Bible passage she chose and we talked together, prayed, and enjoyed each other's company. I visited her each week and she was truly an inspiration. I admired her tenacity and persistence; a caring, compassionate and gentle soul. She was able to look after herself, and cooked with various gadgets for assisting blind people.

One day, she told me with a chuckle that she put tin tomatoes in her pudding bowl instead of peaches! She thrived on her determination, and most certainly her faith in God. She recorded her news, songs, and bible verses on the old-fashioned cassette tapes, and sent them in the post instead of letters! Though I moved away from where Amelia lived, we kept in touch, sending each other recordings on cassette tapes. It was always a joy to receive and fun to make!

30 years later, I am sitting in the church where she once attended. It was the day of her funeral. She was in a nursing home for a few years, died aged 102! Certainly, our loss, but Heaven's gain. We mourn, but are very grateful that through our Lord Jesus Christ and knowing Him, we will meet again one day. I recognised people at the funeral from many years ago. All looking much older; me too of course!

READY...GO!

One thing is certain; how quickly time passes. There is always a challenge at funerals to remember this life on earth is but a vapour; a puff in the light of eternity. Spray a puff from an aerosol can into the air! That is the reality of our days. Sobering. My life, your life. We have today. Who knows if tomorrow will come? God loves you; He wants you to know His full abundant life, health and peace.

"I tell you, now is the time of God's favour, now is the day of salvation."

2 Corinthians 6:2 (NIV).

I want to make my life count for the Kingdom for the spreading of the Gospel. To know Him, love Him, serve Him and make Him known.

"Why, you do not even know what will happen tomorrow. What is your life? You are a mist that appears for a little while, and then vanishes."

James 4:14 (NIV).

Complete the mission God has for you. You are commissioned. GO! Amelia lived and proclaimed Jesus in her home and wherever she went. She imparted to me something very precious as I visited her and came away with far more than I was giving!

Now is the time! How is God commissioning YOU?

_____
_____
_____

READY...GO!

_____
_____
_____
_____

READY...GO!

Chapter 20

Remember who you are!

Our self-image is most influential in the whole of life. It is not an introspective thing to think about who you are, as it will affect all your relationships and life. I was a student in my early 30s studying at Kingdom Faith Bible College in Thwing, Yorkshire. God made a way for me to have 6 months off work to study for two terms at the college. I was excited to be a mature student on a Discipleship Training Course! Being a self-employed nursery manager, God graciously supplied wonderful staff in my absence to supervise the running of the nursery whilst I was away! New adventures begin!

In my first week at college, I encountered the powerful revelation of knowing who I am *in Christ Jesus.* Every session, every day, during the first week, we heard *in Christ* teachings. I have never heard it before, but it transformed my life! It was like a light coming on after 14 years of being a Christian; many of those years feeling defeated, insecure, lacking confidence and inadequate.

> **Knowing the truth of how God sees me *in* Christ Jesus is life changing.**

The dynamics of being with 20 other students on the course was an inspiration. We encouraged each other, and spoke the truth to each other of who we are, as we lived together in a large community house.

What does it mean to be *in Christ Jesus?*

READY…GO!

"I have been crucified with Christ, it is no longer I who live, but Christ lives in me."

Galatians 2:20 (NKJV).

As much as we know the truth, is as much as we will know freedom. Lies must be replaced with truth. Lies we have spoken over ourselves, lies other people have spoken over us and lies of the enemy. Satan's primary weapon is lies!

"If you abide in My word, you are My disciples indeed. And you shall know the truth, and the truth shall make you free."

John 8:31-32 (NKJV).

As Adam and Eve knew each other in their oneness, so understanding and intimate knowledge with the truth will set us free. The Word of God is seed. It grows and strongholds are broken and our minds are renewed. Emotional hurts are healed. Jesus died for our freedom. On our journey, we discover more of our freedom as we encounter Him, and are set free by the truth. It is good to often repeat these words to remind us: *"I am who God says I am, and I can do what God says I can do!"*

There are many references in the New Testament of being *in Christ*. Ephesians has 35! We are brought into union with Him; we are put *in* Christ. To be in Christ is an end to our old self. God no longer sees our imperfections. When He looks at you, He sees Jesus. He sees the righteousness of His own Son. We co-reign with Christ now.

"For you died, and your life is hidden with Christ in God."

Colossians 3:3 (NKJV).

READY…GO!

You are special; God chose you and knew you before the world began!

"For He chose us in Him before the creation of the world to be Holy and blameless in His sight."

Ephesians 1:4 (NIV).

It is powerful to personalise these *in Christ* scriptures. Affirm your identity. Speak it out. "I am chosen, I am blameless." Here are a few other personalised confessions of being in Christ Jesus:

- *"I am a new creation in Christ. The old has passed away. All things have become new."*
- *"God raised me up with Christ and seated me with Him in the Heavenly realms in Christ Jesus."*
- *"In Him, I have faith to approach God with freedom and confidence."*
- *"I am marked in Him with a seal, the promised Holy Spirit; a deposit guaranteeing my inheritance."*

What a joy to share in Christ's inheritance! We are not alone, but living in Him. Some counselling points us too deeply into ourselves. What we need is a *truth* encounter of who we are in Christ; that is, we died and are raised to new life with a new nature! I remember in my early days as a Christian, I was struggling with various issues. I went to see the Pastor and he read out loud to me God's Word from Romans. It was a truth encounter. My identity is who God says I am. I can live in victory and freedom. Don't let anyone steal your identity!

"God has not given us a spirit of fear, but of power and of love and of a sound mind."

2 Timothy 1:7 (NKJV).

READY…GO!

Knowing our identity in Christ is life transforming. If you don't know who you are, you won't *do* what you can do! I have a set of four Russian stacking dolls that were among the toys at Acorn Nursery. God showed me to use them as a visual aid for this revelation! In descending order of size are God the Father, Jesus, you, and Holy Spirit.

It is a powerful, visible demonstration as I place the Holy Spirit in you; you are placed *in* Christ Jesus, and when Father God looks at you, He sees Jesus! As leaders, it touches the people we lead. We receive our identity from God alone. Remember who you are! Our standing before God is perfect in Christ. We walk our journey with Him, relying on His grace as we *'act justly, love mercy, and walk humbly with our God.' – Micah 6:8 (NIV)*.

What impact does being chosen by God have on your life? Meditate on your identity in Christ Jesus:

_____
_____
_____
_____
_____
_____

READY…GO!

Chapter 21

Mum

I always enjoyed a train journey, but on this journey to Poole, I was thinking about Mum. She was in a hospice. I watched rolling hills and beautiful countryside out of the window. It was a lovely September, sunny day. My destination was near. I saw Poole Harbour sparkling in the sunshine. After a 4-hour journey, I got a taxi to the hospice.

Mum was sitting on a chair in her room; Dad besides her. She had been at the hospice for a few days. I gave them a big hug. It was not long before Dad said, "So, the round robin prayers didn't work then?" I replied, "So long as you know where you're going, you'll be alright." Then I said to Mum, "If you died tonight, would you be sure you are going to heaven?" She replied, "No." I said, "Shall we pray then?" She responded, "Yes."

I asked her to repeat the Salvation prayer line by line after me. (Something like the prayer in the Introduction). She prayed and gave her life to God that day at the age of 83! I said to her, "There; you are born again!" She repeated the words "born again" as though she had heard them before, and now understood the meaning for the first time! Maybe she had heard it at Sunday School a long time ago.

Before I left the following day to return home, the three of us held hands in a circle. I prayed for God's blessing and peace in the hospice. It was a great comfort to me. She only had a few more days of consciousness. God's timing is perfect. I returned to the Railway Station feeling sad. I knew I wouldn't see her again in this life, but rejoiced that she found her Saviour, and I am at peace. I heard the sound of the train tracks in the distance. My journey home began. I relaxed and watched the world go by as I looked out of the window.

READY...GO!

My thoughts drifted, and I thanked God for His amazing love and kindness, and His gift of eternal life. I thanked Him for answered prayers for mum. Seeds sown throughout the years. Our physical death is a gateway into eternity. Meanwhile, I pondered Mum's last words to me, "You've got a lot of living to do!" Yes, I want to make the most of the remainder of my life to serve the One who gives me life in abundance!

It is the best privilege, joy, and honour to lead Mum to the Lord. She had not put her trust in God until that point. The Chaplain of the hospice visited her and they read some Bible verses together. It turned out to be just a week before she died. It was amazing to be part of someone's eternal destiny, especially in your family!

Mum was the first person I led to the Lord, giving an invitation to pray the salvation prayer. A heart for mission is born! This is 2 weeks into the start of the Mission24 Training Course in evangelism, for which I am forever grateful! It was the birthing of stepping out into unchartered waters to share the Gospel, seeing many give their lives to God. What a joy!

"Believe on the Lord Jesus Christ, and you will be saved; you and your household."

Acts 16:31 (NKJV).

How is God leading you to share the Gospel with family members? God's promise is for you and your household:

_____

_____

_____

_____

_____

READY...GO!

READY...GO!

Chapter 22

Full Steam Ahead!

Sitting on a bench at Ruislip Railway Station, I waited with my brother, Gran and Grandad. I was 4 years old, and on our way to visit famous sights in London! All very exciting! Often, a steam train pulled into the station with loud screeches of brakes. It was a dramatic awe-inspiring sight, even a little scary as a young girl! It looked like a monster hissing and blowing steam!

A glimpse of fire in the firebox. A rumbling of wheels and the smell of steam. I hid my face in Gran's lap to muffle the noise as we sat and waited. We walked to the edge of the platform and climbed on. The fireman kept shovelling coal into the locomotives' firebox. Choo-choo on the whistle; we're off, chugging along, clickety-clack! This was my first experience of steam trains and I loved it! They have not been in railway service since 1968, but of course, there are many preserved railways today where steam train rides still offer great adventure and excitement!

I admire the grandeur of steam trains today, and I sometimes take a ride! As I watched the fireman shovelling coal to keep the engine moving, I realised that it is a skilled job. Actually, it was a fire 'lady' this time; she looked ahead at the terrain to know the speed required, whether it was up or downhill. She assessed where to put the coal in the firebox to build up enough steam pressure to start moving. This process heated the water in the boiler to create steam to power the engine.

There was always something to do as she got ready for what was next! I found it fascinating; as God was speaking to me about prayer. Just as fire drives the engine, our prayers are the engine room and powerhouse for God's plans and purposes in the Church, our lives, families, nations, and the world! Prayer energises us to love God and people. We are created to receive and express the burning love that originates in God's heart, for *"God is love" – 1 John 4:16 (NKJV).*

READY...GO!

Our fervent prayers make way for God to move:

"The effective, fervent prayer of a righteous man avails much."

James 5:16 (NKJV).

Connection to Jesus at heart level through prayer is the lifeline that enables us to sustain what God is calling us to. As our passion is stirred up, and we pray in tongues for extended times, 30 minutes, or an hour, we become more deeply connected with Him, and strengthened. Our prayers rise as incense. We live from our union with God from the throne position. We see the enemy for what he really is, disarmed, and with no legal right to touch any of us.

> **Declare: "I trample on you and render you ineffective!"**

"No weapon formed against you shall prosper, and every tongue which rises against you in judgement, you shall condemn. This is the heritage of the servants of the Lord, and their righteousness is from Me."

Isaiah 54:17 (NKJV).

May God unleash the revelation of who you are in Christ Jesus. We have the power and authority in Him for the pulling down of strongholds:

"We do not war according to the flesh. For the weapons of our warfare are not carnal, but mighty in God for pulling down strongholds, casting down arguments and every high thing that exalts itself against the knowledge of God, bringing every thought into captivity to the obedience of Christ."

2 Corinthians 10:3-5 (NKJV).

READY…GO!

A stronghold is a bondage. We have spiritual weapons to break bondages in our lives, and those we are praying and interceding for. We can speak God's Word over situations; it is living and active. God moves at the sound of our words:

"For the Word of God is living and powerful, and sharper than any two-edge sword, piercing even to the division of soul and spirit."

Hebrews 4:12 (NKJV).

The Name of Jesus is powerful as we pray for healing, deliverance and miracles! I have the joy of praying with Mission24 on Zoom each weekday morning for outreach and missions. We have the delight of seeing much fruit, transformation and lives turned around! A friend and I meet together on video calls each week to pray for our families.

> **God wants to mobilise and use us to mobilise others as the Church rises with authority.**

Hearts surrendered and ignited with fresh fire from the altar of His Presence. God shows me that He wants a fasted lifestyle, rather than fasting for situations; a regular day each week to fast and pray, and for longer periods as God leads.

I recently heard God saying to me, *"Don't stop at basecamp!"* He is calling me to move and meet with Him up the mountain. I heard that it takes 40 days to climb from the basecamp on Mount Everest to the summit, so I was inspired to do a 40-day *virtual* climb with a partial fast; one simple meal a day. Jesus is my Mountain Guide; we walk and talk together. As I draw close and listen to His heart each day, journalling our time together; I am thankful for a very special 40-day journey! Let's partner with Him to release His Presence and resources into the earth.

READY...GO!

Get on board the engine room of prayer! Let's GO! Is God challenging you in any way?

_____
_____
_____
_____
_____
_____
_____

READY…GO!

Chapter 23

Tightrope Walk!

Clowns, trapeze acts and jugglers are among the performers at circuses. The ringmaster introduces the next act. There were tense moments as I watched the skill of a tightrope walker wavering along a thin wire, high up in the Big Top Circus tent, carrying a long flexi pole for balance. Music played and there were lights and dazzling acrobats on the tightrope as the crowds sat on the edge of their seats!

When I first gave my life to God, I carried a belief that my life was like a tightrope walk! Each step forward, I perceived to be a precarious balancing act, cautiously moving forwards to make sure I don't fall off the path! Unknowingly, I believed the lie that God is a strict taskmaster. It robbed me of the identity He wanted to give me. He is far more loving and gracious than ever I imagine! I hear His reassuring words and affirmation. He says:

"I will guide you, instruct you and set your pace. I carry the load and give you peace and rest. Not like a tightrope walker! I walk beside you. Accept My will. Trust My timing. I bring healing and restoration. You will know the truth of who I am and who you are. I do not rule over you as if you were a robot needing to be programmed for every detail of its activity. I teach you to daily yield and move with Me. Be free within My Lordship to follow your heart without condemnation. I trust you; that trust comes from a relationship of love and commitment. You are yoked to Me; that yoke fits perfectly! There is no burden to carry; only rest, and contentment as you walk with Me. We shall do mighty exploits!"

Being yoked with Jesus is beautiful; nothing like a tightrope walk! A yoke is a wooden beam, sometimes used between a pair of oxen or other animals to enable them to pull together on a load. A wonderful picture of walking side by side with Jesus; close and

READY...GO!

intimate! A posture of surrender and trust as He shapes us into His image.

"Come to Me, all you who labour and are heavy laden, and I will give you rest. Take My yoke upon you and learn from Me, for I am gentle and lowly in heart, and you will find rest for your souls. For My yoke is easy and My burden is light."

Matthew 11:28-30 (NKJV).

Just as a farmer puts a yoke on his livestock, commonly donkeys, mules and oxen, so we allow Jesus to direct us in all we do to learn from Him. Yoked with Him at His pace. We don't need to carry the weight; we move forwards in the same direction as Jesus. That is what we are created for; to be joined with Him in freedom and ease. Come to Jesus every day in prayer and reading the Word. He gives direction, rest and peace. He invites us. Keep seeking Him. Meet with other believers. It was said of Uzziah:

"He sought God during the days of Zechariah who instructed Him in the fear of God. As long as He sought the Lord, God gave him success."

2 Chronicles 26:5 (NIV).

It is important to speak God's perspective and declare life, not death. There is power in our words:

"Death and life are in the power of the tongue, and those who love it will eat its fruit."

Proverbs 18:21 (NKJV).

READY...GO!

Ask God if there is any area in your life where you are not believing the truth of who God really is. Replace the lies with truth and write them below:

_____
_____
_____
_____
_____
_____
_____

READY...GO!

Chapter 24

Heart to Heart

I leaned forwards picturing Jesus sitting next to me. I am holding my physical heart in my hands and I give it to Jesus. He puts it inside His heart! I see He is wearing a jacket, opens it and puts it inside. A wonderful, intimate vision. It seemed timeless. I have a strong sense He is enjoying every moment. He takes great pleasure in having my heart next to His. He says to me; "You'll need your heart back now!" I sensed His reluctance to let it go and I reached out to take it. As I did, I experienced immediate healing of stomach irritations! He showed me the reality of the encounter.

It is wonderful and amazing! I am His and He is mine. He says: "I take your heart. You present it to Me; a soft heart. I have great pleasure in putting your heart next to mine! I have been working on it. A beautiful heart, tenderised and regulated according to My heart beat. Never the same again. Recalibrated with My heart beat and in tune with My rhythm. A heart after Me. A surrendered heart."

This encounter with Jesus profoundly transformed me. Particularly, the truth that He actually *enjoys* having my heart next to His. He loves, accepts and created me. I am God's work of art, His poem! His workmanship!

"For we are His workmanship created in Christ Jesus for good works which God prepared beforehand that we should walk in them."

Ephesians 2:10 (NKJV).

God loves to see us swimming in His love, free to be who He created us to be. He has a plan for you that is full of hope, purpose and beauty. He wants you to discover it. Sometimes, we find ourselves mishearing according to previous experiences. I hear Him saying:

READY…GO!

"Do not label yourself or let others label you. When I died on the Cross, I had you in my heart. I saw the brokenness, the fallen nature and longed to restore to you all that was lost in the Garden. To restore the brokenness, turn fear to faith, turmoil to peace, lack to plenty, and anguish to fulfilment in Me. Stand up and claim what is yours! It is paid for! Go! Touch the throne of Heaven, and you will touch the earth with My goodness. Arise in your God-given destiny."

The Truth transforms us and the world around us. I also hear God saying: "You are not and never were responsible for the way you were treated and misused. I loose you! No more blame, discouragement or shame. Come back to *life* again."

You are created to receive and express the burning love that originates in God's heart:

"And we have known and believed the love that God has for us. God is love and he who abides in love abides in God, and God in him."

1 John 4:16 (NKJV).

God uses failure in our lives to fulfil His perfect plan. Our journey can be terrifying, but He wants you free! Your purpose is birthed from intimacy with the King. We can have intimacy in communion. Christians have taken communion since the early days of the church, and it is a beautiful heart-to-heart connection with the King, remembering what Jesus did on the Cross. It can be at home or anywhere! As you relate to people, heart-to-heart, it is the *real* you that impacts others. Heart to heart in the King's Presence always brings healing:

"Above all else, guard your heart, for it is the wellspring of life."

Proverbs 4:23 (NKJV).

READY...GO!

Above all else, earnestly desire that heart-to-heart relationship with the King. Picture yourself sitting with Jesus. What is He saying to you?

_____

_____

_____

_____

_____

_____

_____

READY...GO!

Chapter 25

Wake Up!

One beep of the fire alarm! A high-pitched sound; it immediately got my attention. I was jolted awake at 3.00am! There was no fire, just a low battery in the fire alarm! I hear the Spirit of God saying: "A different sound in the Spirit realm is coming. People will wake up immediately and it will catch their attention. It is a spiritual awakening; people will wake up from their slumber. They will see reality and turn their eyes to Me.

It is time to wake up! You will see clarity. You will see in the Spirit realm before you see in the physical realm. I entrust you with much. Listen and pay attention to My promptings. You have insights and wisdom to give away. I give you new glasses; you will see the way ahead. I give you creativities in My Kingdom. My Word is life and will explode in your midst. I am your Creator God. I live in you! I love to create."

As you write your thoughts and impressions, it will become a two-way dialogue of connection with God. Press in. Position yourself and expect God to speak to you. He will! He may show you a picture, a scripture, or maybe you are sensing God's heart through real life experiences. What is He showing you for yourself and for others?

I am excited that many who have not yet turned to God will *hear* the alarm and give their lives to Him. We pray and intercede for hearts to be awoken. God longs to pour out His love and mercy in a broken world:

"Blow the trumpet in Zion, and sound an alarm in My Holy Mountain! Let all the inhabitants of the land tremble; for the day of the Lord is coming."

Joel 2:1 (NKJV).

READY...GO!

The ram's horn known as the shofar, was used to herald impending danger. Also, to call the assembly together:

"Consecrate a fast, call a sacred assembly; gather the elders, and all the inhabitants of the land into the house of the Lord your God, and cry out to the Lord."

Joel 1:14 (NKJV).

As we pray and fast, and cry out to the Lord in desperation, He hears and answers. He awakens us to the larger purposes He has of reaching the world around us through the power and the work of His Spirit.

"And it shall come to pass afterward that I will pour out My Spirit on all flesh; your sons and daughters shall prophesy, your old men shall dream dreams, and young men shall see visions. And also, on My menservants and on My maidservants, I will pour out My Spirit in those days."

Joel 2:28-29 (NKJV).

Salvation will arise for all those who call upon the Name of the Lord as they witness God's Spirit at work in His people.

"And it shall come to pass that whoever calls on the Name of the Lord shall be saved."

Joel 2:32 (NKJV).

God speaks to us in the midst of difficulties. His Word sustains and enables us to focus on Him. The word God put in my heart in the pandemic lockdown was *"Look to the horizon."* In the restrictions

READY...GO!

of the season, in the isolation and job loss, illness and grief, God stills my heart.

I positioned myself to *see* beyond the four walls of my home. I took short walks most days to the back entrance of a large National Trust country house; usually open to the public set in acres of parkland. I looked to the horizon through the large chained and padlocked gate to the house at the end of a long straight track.

As I looked beyond myself, I was at peace and rest! Looking to the horizon gives me hope. Seeing with an eternal perspective always brings freedom. It was a delight when the padlocked gates were open once again. I stepped in to the reality of what I could only *see* from a distance through the bars of the locked gates. A beautiful sunny day with deer running around, lots of sheep and stunning countryside!

God calls us to be awake to make the most of every opportunity. Keep listening to His voice and walk in the light:

"Awake, you who sleep, arise from the dead and Christ will give you light."

Ephesians 5:14 (NKJV).

We need to be alert and watchful, paying attention to what is going on in our lives and in the world around us. We need to be wise to the schemes of the enemy.

"Be self-controlled and alert. Your enemy the devil prowls around like a roaring lion looking for someone to devour. Resist him, standing firm in the faith, because you know that your brothers throughout the world are undergoing the same kind of sufferings."

1 Peter 5:8-9 (NIV).

READY...GO!

Finally, I pictured a princess asleep. In children's tales, she was woken by a kiss! I hear the Lord saying, "Wake up! I kiss you with dew from Heaven. Be released into all My goodness and know My refreshing."

Is God calling you to be awake in a new way?

_____
_____
_____
_____
_____
_____
_____

READY...GO!

Chapter 26

Raise the Flag!

As a Girl Guide, I remembered being chosen to carry the Guide flag on parade. It was quite heavy. I learnt how to carry it, positioning my hands in a certain way around the pole, holding it at the correct angle! I felt honoured to be chosen to carry it; it fluttered in the breeze. All the Girl Guides assembled and walked in twos along the street and into the church.

We often saw multitudes of flags at royal processions and occasions. They were originally used in warfare as rallying points for people to gather, or for signalling. Flags can be used for decoration and display. They are a symbol of identity, unity, and convey messages of shared purpose. Children love to wave flags at parties and position them on top of sandcastles on the beach! Children often ask me to make one at nursery with paper and a straw! We see flags in parades, football games and on poles outside homes and businesses. The design of the flag is unique to its particular identity.

My attention is turned to flags and banners in praise and worship to our God. We see a flag on a royal residence to show that the King or Queen is actually in residence at that moment! We raise high the flags to exalt our God and King; to celebrate Him. One of the Names of God is Jehovah-Nissi, which means *"The Lord is my Banner."* Moses built an altar and called it Jehovah-Nissi after the Israelites had defeated the Amalekites in battle in reference to Exodus 17:15. A victory banner!

God is our banner of love and protection. Banners and flags today are a beautiful, visible and prophetic sign of the Spirit. Many churches have banners and flags to express worship to God in a visual way. Knowing who we are and how much we are loved, we extravagantly worship the King of Kings. We celebrate His victory and know that God is our rallying point; He gives strength for the battle.

READY...GO!

"We will shout for joy when you are victorious and will lift up our banners in the Name of our God. May the Lord grant all your requests."

Psalm 20:5 (NIV).

Worship; connecting with our Creator is joy filled! The significance of flags is that they symbolise God's promises and faithfulness. I made three flags in the colours of red, gold and blue! The flags were made with sheer fabric, hemmed with an iron-on hem tape and dowel rod for the pole! Simple! I used them in church gatherings and worship at home. Children at Messy Church and Rhyme Time loved them too!

The colours of the flags are a visual demonstration of spiritual truth. The red flag symbolises the Blood of Jesus; the gold; His Kingship, and the blue; His refreshing, healing waters. As we lift high the flags in praise, we also stake our claim in prayer for ourselves, our families and beyond. The position of a flag can be half-mast on a building, ship or on the land. This is a mark of respect for a person who has died. We do not want to be half-mast or half-hearted as we give the living God all the Worship He deserves! It is a beautiful truth that we live under the banner of love and intimacy with the King!

"He brought me to the banqueting house, and His banner over me was love."

Song of Solomon 2:4 (NKJV).

While leading Rhyme Time in church, a group for pre-school children and parents, we usually finished with parachute play. A parachute is like a banner! God showed me to pray over it, and as we each held the edge of the parachute, God's peace and Presence were tangible!

READY...GO!

One of my poems expressing the *joy* of worship:

Worship:
To worship You is pure delight,
Such joy to know our sins forgiven,
That precious blood, it freely flows,
Restores us to our God in Heaven.
Oh, Holy God, our hearts are one,
To You, Oh Lord, our hands we raise,
We fix our eyes on You alone
And give to You our highest praise!

"He has put a new song in my mouth, praise to our God; many will see it and fear, and will trust in the Lord."

Psalm 40:3 (NKJV).

Reflect on your lifestyle of worship. Let a new song arise:

_____
_____
_____
_____
_____
_____
_____

Chapter 27

Do you hear the Drum Beat?

A sound from Heaven touching earth. A sound touching my heart is drawing me close into God's Presence. Drumming to the heart beat of God in prayer and worship. I feel alive in heart-to-heart connection; deeper than words. I almost stumbled across this amazing gift of the bongo drums! A box I never opened.

I bought them to use at a children's group, and took out the bongos and began to play. A complete novice! Bongos are an Afro-Cuban percussion instrument; a pair of small, open drums of different sizes. By using your fingers and different strokes of your hand, a variety of sounds are played.

I hear the Lord saying: "The war drums are beating in Heaven. They beat as My heart is grieved by what I see the enemy doing to My people and Creation. I see the suffering. Know this; victory is sure! There will be rescues because of your prayers. Angels are released. Keep worshipping, keep warring, keep pursuing and keep drumming. There are miracles in My Presence. Proclaim the Kingdom of God in your midst. Worship and praise. Chains break at the sound. There is a rattling. Where you have been locked in, pushed down, buried, abandoned and abused, I say rise up!"

As I was praying with a friend on a video call, I saw a large angel in the clouds behind her! The amazing thing was that I actually spoke about angels at the time!

"Bless the Lord, you His angels, who excel in strength, who do His Word, heeding the voice of His Word."

Psalm 103:20 (NKJV).

READY...GO!

When we speak God's Word, angels start working. I saw a long drainpipe from heaven to earth blocked with rubbish, blocking God's provision. Then, a rush of water came through it to clear the way. It was as if the angel was blowing through it! Thank you, Lord for signs and wonders!

God wants us to rise up! I wasn't particularly naughty as a young child; however, on occasions, I remember being locked in my bedroom with a bolt on the outside as punishment for something I must have done. Around the age of 4, this was not a pleasant experience. God brings it to light and I realise it probably had an impact into my adult years of feeling hemmed in and trapped. God brings freedom and wholeness, and release from trauma as *roots from the past are pulled up and broken off.*

He reassures me that He was there, and Father God lovingly picks me up. I can release forgiveness. Allow God to show you any trauma in your past that is hindering you; even now. *Speak death to what needs to die.* Speak death to the trauma that can sometimes turn into illness in your physical body. Pull up the roots of those things from the past that do not belong in your future. God makes all things new. You can rise again!

So, God is encouraging me to be steadfast in prayer, play the bongos in worship, warfare and intercession. God says: "Release your sound!" *Be a voice, not an echo.* The sound is where there is breakthrough. God loves to hear our voice, our sound, talking, singing and communing with Him.

"My dove in the clefts of the rock, in the hiding places on the mountainside, show me your face, let me hear your voice; for your voice is sweet, and your face is lovely."

Song of Songs 2:14 (NIV).

I hear the Spirit of the Lord saying: "Write songs of your heart. Songs to soothe. When you sing, your voice carries My breath in the

READY...GO!

airwaves, cutting through darkness, demonic chaos and thoughts. It brings alignment in the spirit over many lives."

As I pray and worship in a family members house, I knew that the buddha statues had to go that were brought from travels abroad. They are more than simple ornaments; they represent worship of idols and are not honouring to God. He made a way for me to remove them and pray for cleansing.

> **Ask God to reveal anything in your home that isn't from Him.**

I am often singing, especially around children as it brings peace and stillness! We sing a welcome song at the beginning of Rhyme Time to each individual child. It is powerful with the words "God bless you" in it! It pronounces God's blessing on them and their families. I feel the conviction of the Holy Spirit one day on my way to Rhyme Time. He says: "You can't do Rhyme Time without a song in your heart!" True, that morning, I didn't have a song in my heart. I repented and asked God to fill me again! God inhabits the praises of His people! We can sing songs of deliverance! The bongos are truly an instrument of praise!

Let God highlight anything from your past including any trauma that is hindering you. Break off the roots, in Jesus' Name. Amen! Enter into freedom:

_____
_____
_____
_____
_____
_____

READY…GO!

Chapter 28

Cry from the Heart

The woman sat alone in a world of her own, her head bowed down. She was weary of her futile ways; all was meaningless. How could she go on? Her eyes were dim; no spark of life. She felt the evils of her heart. The battles inside were raging. She had nowhere to turn, nowhere to go. What could she offer to the world outside? *The story continues:*

All she sees is her inadequacy, her blackness and barrenness. Who will bother with someone like her? Who will listen to her heart's cry? Who will love this one? Who will care? Why would they in this self-sufficient world? Her heart was heavy. The rejection and guilt locked her into her own dark world.

The woman got up and looked out of the window. "Is there anyone out there who understands?" It was her heart's cry. She overheard a conversation in the street. She learnt that Jesus was coming to a house nearby for dinner. Many thoughts rushed through her mind, and hope began to rise. She wasted no time; she found a jar of precious perfume. Quickly, she made her way to the house, tightly clutching the jar in her hand. Her mind invaded with many distractions, but her heart set on reaching her destination. Her eyes were glassy. She had a lump in her throat. She hurried; nothing else mattered.

"Jesus, Jesus!" she cried and fell to her knees. Tears began to flood down her cheeks. Tears of remorse, tears of love poured out from her longing heart. Is this true love at last? Will this man turn her away? His feet became wet with her tears. She wiped them with her hair and kissed them. "Jesus, Jesus!" she cried as she poured perfume on His feet. She looked into His eyes and her heart melted. That gentle smile says "My child; I understand."

READY...GO!

She sees in Him her only hope. "Here I am; I lay myself and all that I am at Your feet. Here I am; worthless, yet; You are so Worthy." Jesus looked at the woman. He sees her heart. He sees her faith. He says: "Come, rise up my child!" He does not condemn her, but is full of compassion. "Your sins are forgiven. Go in peace!" She is overwhelmed by His love. She rises up. Her thankful heart finds peace and rest at last. She is free; her sins are forgiven. She meets the life-giver, now to live in the Kingdom of God; a high calling indeed!

This is a story I wrote many years ago in the early days of reaching out to God myself; picturing myself as that woman. The outline of the story is based on Luke 7:36-50. I have also used it as a short drama sketch. God is faithful. I have never looked back. He brings healing and salvation, purpose, hope, worth and dignity. With open arms, He says *"Come!"*

When you know who you belong to, you come alive!

We can be channels to see God move in other people's lives. Those who are discouraged and see the future as a black hole. They don't know how God can help; those who feel rejected and criticised or put down. There are those who feel condemned, lonely, confused, hurt and wounded. They are bleeding inside and need someone to heal the pain. Jesus says:

"The Spirit of the Lord is upon Me because He has anointed Me to preach the Gospel to the poor; He has sent me to heal the broken-hearted, to proclaim liberty to the captives and recovery of sight to the blind, to set at liberty those who are oppressed; to proclaim the acceptable year of the Lord."

Luke 4:18 (NKJV).

READY...GO!

Jesus passes this same ministry on to His disciples and ultimately, to the entire church! READY...GO! Consider how and where God wants you to GO! You are anointed and appointed as a Disciple of Christ!

_____
_____
_____
_____
_____
_____
_____

READY...GO!

Chapter 29

A Mirage!

The wind howled furiously. There was nothing in sight as the man battled the wind in the vast desolation of the rippling desert sands. He must keep going. He cannot turn back. A gust of wind blew sand into his face; the storm raged. He began questioning his commission. "Why did I ever begin this long endless journey? It's too hard! How can I make it?" He was very tired and thirsty; that first spurt of enthusiasm was gone.

He looked at his water supply, "How long will it last?" He looked around. "Is there anyone out there?" Maybe the comfort of a fellow traveller will help him along the way. He turned to the side as something in the distance attracted his attention. "Is it a resting place, a shelter in the storm? There, I can fill up with water for the journey." *My dream continues:*

The man puts all his effort into following the diversion off the Straight Way. He was eager to get to the oasis. He was almost there and ready to take his ease. This pathway seemed so much harder, and more demanding. He got closer, but to his utter dismay, as he approached, he found that it was only a mirage. His heart sank. He felt it was the end. "Surely, I will die." So much time wasted; he needed to get back on track. He resolved never again to chase after attractions and fantasies.

Even though the Way would not always be easy, he reaffirmed his vow to follow the Highway, not sideroads that only lead to frustration and emptiness. The Lord says:

"I will provide all you need for your journey. Each day, I am your provider. Do not worry about tomorrow. Fix your eyes on Me. Though other things may attract you, resist the temptation. Do not put your hope in false attractions; things that fade away. I am the Rock. I am your security and comfort in the storm. Do not run away

READY...GO!

and hide; call on My name. My Grace is sufficient for you. Trust Me for each new day. Drink from Me the pure living waters. They never run dry."

God speaks in dreams. I had a dream about this mirage in the desert; hence the story that I subsequently wrote! God speaks powerfully of His strength and provision through hard and difficult times. He is faithful and calls us to keep going. His resources are infinite!

God draws us close to Himself, especially in the difficult seasons. It is a time and space for God to work, emptied of trivia and false directions.

> **Only those content with God can be satisfied in the wilderness.**

It is a time of aloneness with Him. He makes our *"Valley of Achor, a door of hope."* Achor means *trouble*. God redeems situations, bringing hope in the place of previous trouble.

"Therefore, I am now going to allure her; I will lead her into the desert and speak tenderly to her. There, I will give her back her vineyards, and will make the Valley of Achor a door of hope. There, she will sing as in the days of her youth, as in the day she came up out of Egypt."

Hosea 21:14-15 (NIV).

How is God transforming your Valley of Achor into a door of hope?

_____

_____

_____

READY…GO!

READY...GO!

Chapter 30

The Way of the Lord

Teach me, Oh Lord to follow You,
Where You go, there will I go,
And where You stay, so will I stay,
Your ways I long to know.

I ask dear Lord for a heart that's true,
Faithful I'll ever be,
Direct my path in the way of life,
For there is liberty.

I ask Oh Lord for a single heart
That never turns away,
For You have died and paid the price,
Prepared for us the way.

Turn my eyes from worthless things,
From all that would call me away,
I will go on for Jesus' sake,
I'll hasten and not delay.

Jesus alone is all my life,
Your Kingdom Lord, I love,
All else is but a passing mist,
I'll seek those things above.

Jesus alone is the one true Rock
From a thankful heart, I'll sing,
Jesus, my Lord, my life, my all,
Accept the praise I bring.

This poem encompasses my pursuit of God, asking Him to teach me and show me the way ahead. It is more than 40 years since writing it! He is faithful and worthy of all the praise! A lifetime of learning,

READY...GO!

every day is a school day! Learning to be patient with myself, remaining teachable, and having the courage to get up and go on when the going gets tough. God gives faithful friends who are always there. There are seasons of loss, disappointment and ill health, but God is a God of restoration.

"I will repay you for the years the locusts have eaten, the great locust and the young locust, the other locusts and the locust swarm, my great army that I sent among you. You will have plenty to eat until you are full, and you will praise the Name of the Lord your God, who has worked wonders for you; never again will My people be shamed."

Joel 2:25-26 (NIV).

God is the One who defeats our enemies. He provides the ability to bear much fruit. He wants to restore every broken place in our lives, and in the lives of those we are praying for. Full restoration of fruit and harvest that the locusts have eaten. God gives back in a wonderful way as we reclaim what the enemy has stolen:

"The thief does not come except to steal, and to kill, and to destroy. I have come that they may have life, and that they may have it more abundantly."

John 10:10 (NKJV).

Abundant life! That's God's intention from the very beginning of time. He wants us to be filled with joy. God made everything and declared it to be good! He wanted to share that dominion with us. Jesus restores to us what was lost through Adam and Eve in the Garden of Eden. We can experience a superabundant, overflowing, more than enough, extraordinary life!

READY...GO!

"Restore us, Oh God; cause your face to shine and we shall be saved."

Psalm 80:3 (NKJV).

To shine means to smile. A beautiful picture, God sees us and smiles! God restores the years the locusts have eaten. How is God doing that for you?

_____
_____
_____
_____
_____
_____
_____

READY…GO!

Chapter 31

Garden of Delights

I heard the Lord say: "You are a beautiful flower at the side of a dry dusty track. A few other flowers dotted here and there. You look to see who is coming. No-one has the time to stop in the heat of the day. As people pass by, the dust rises and settles along the edge of the track on the flowers. You feel insignificant, and you question your existence in this barren, dry place. Know this; you have a special place in My heart. I know you and see your questions. I placed you there. If the sole reason for being there is that it brings pleasure to Me, then accept this. I delight in you.

I have a greater purpose for you. Do not despise these times, for you are becoming stronger, straight and upright as you reach for the sun through the dust. In My time, you will be planted in a fertile garden. Many flowers all around you; all colours and sizes, a well-tended garden. I place you with other flowers that complement and enhance the flower that you are; indeed, your place among them makes the garden a beautiful fragrance to Me. A garden of delights!

People come, look and ponder on the beauty of the garden; it is buzzing with life. They no longer hurry past as they linger in My Presence. I ordain this; I choose you to be part of this delightful garden to minister life to those who are thirsty."

God showed me this *picture* of the dusty track, then the garden. I am reminded that gardens are subject to different seasons of the year. We have different seasons in our walk with God. Sometimes, it feels like we're on the edge of a dry, dusty track. He says: "Rise up! You do not belong in the dust, but remember that out of the dust, I formed life. I breathe My life and My breath into you."

A beautiful flower I admire is the edelweiss in the mountains of Austria. However, some of them may not ever be seen by the human

READY...GO!

eye; yet, they proudly display their beauty! How wonderfully we can display the Father's Glory, and bring pleasure to Him!

In tough seasons, it is good to remember "it came to pass!" It will end. God accomplishes a lot in our lives in those dry and dusty seasons that He can't do in any other way. God places us in a body of believers, each purchased by the Precious Blood of Christ, and each one unique to serve God in a variety of ways. Each flower complements and enhances the others. Truly, a garden of delights!

"No longer will they call you Deserted, or name your land Desolate. But you will be called Hephzibah, and your land Beulah, for the Lord will take delight in you, and your land will be married."

Isaiah 62:4 (NIV).

Hephzibah means *my delight is in her,* and Beulah means *married,* these names signify God's restoration. We are not deserted or desolate. God longs to meet with us in our *garden* as we invite Him in.

"May your awakening breath blow upon my life until I am fully yours. Breathe upon me with your Spirit-wind. Stir up the sweet spice of your life within me. Spare nothing as you make me your fruitful garden. Hold nothing back until I release your fragrance. Come walk with me as you walked with Adam in your paradise garden. Come, taste the fruits of your life in me."

Song of Songs 4:16 (TPT).

Unfold our future, Lord, as a flower unfurling in the sun. Full surrender to You. A perfect, sweet-smelling fragrance; delightful! Much fruit and seed bearing in Your garden of delights, drawing others to our Creator God.

READY...GO!

Ask God to "blow on your garden." Invite Him in to your garden of delights. What is He saying to you?

_____

_____

_____

_____

_____

_____

_____

READY...GO!

Chapter 32

Sails to the Wind

A clipper ship in full sail; a beautiful and majestic sight. It's built for speed. Each sail aligned and set to the wind. The tall, sturdy, oak masts, strong and enduring. There is something profound about a clipper ship that touches me deeply, particularly since bringing a prophetic word about a clipper ship at the church I was in at the time!

I hear the Spirit of the Lord saying: "I am preparing the ship, the sails. I am preparing My body to respond to the moving of a mighty wind; each sail aligned and ready for the outpouring of My Holy Spirit. The ship is on the move, ready to advance, ready to GO! The tide is right, the prevailing wind blows. Each small sail is important and realigned. Anchors pulled up, ropes untied, the ship launches with speed and grace.

Nothing can stop it now! It glides through deep waters. Great anticipation and excitement. My Spirit is moving powerfully, freeing you as you break loose into the ocean to catch many fish. You can go into the deep where little boats cannot go. Put up your sail in all your vulnerability, and align with others, teamwork.

Let Me guide you in unchartered waters. A fresh wind blows, divine life and energy empowering you to do what you could never have done before! Limitations are broken off and fear is broken. There is breakthrough. Something has to break! There is a fresh wind."

I see the clipper ship as the whole body of Christ; the Bride of Christ coming together as never before. Walls and divisions coming down and new territories of God's Kingdom expanding into the deep to catch multitudes of fish. After the miraculous catch of the multitude of fish, Jesus reminds His disciples, *"Do not be afraid. From now on, you will catch men"* in reference to Luke 5:10 (NKJV).

READY...GO!

Churches are coming together for mission, to reach communities and share the gospel. Change happens when the wind blows; the direction is changing and the Holy Spirit is moving. The breath of God transforms us into a mighty force for God.

This is a powerful prayer as we ask God to transform us; by Sir. Francis Drake; a great navigator, seaman and explorer in 1577:

Disturb us, Lord when
We are too well pleased with ourselves
When our dreams have come true
Because we dreamed too little,
When we arrived safely
Because we sailed too close to the shore.

Disturb us, Lord when
With the abundance of things we possess
We have lost our thirst
For the Waters of life,
We have ceased to dream of eternity
And in our efforts to build a new earth,
We have allowed our vision
Of the new Heaven to dim.

Disturb us, Lord to dare more boldly,
To venture on wider seas
Where storms will show your mastery;
Where losing sight of land
We shall find the stars.

We ask you to push back
The horizons of our hopes;
And to push us in the future
In strength, courage, hope and love.

READY...GO!

'Disturb us, Lord.' Receive the fresh wind of the Holy Spirit. How can we venture on wider seas with other believers?

READY…GO!

Chapter 33

Tent Pegs!

The wind was whistling around the campsite. The rain poured relentlessly. A stormy night, a frightening noise as the wind frantically pulled at the guy ropes on my little tent. It was in the middle of the night at Grapevine; an annual Christian celebration on the Lincolnshire Showground over August bank holiday weekend, in the late 80's. Will the tent pegs hold? Will they remain secure through the storm? I pray! I love to camp, make memories, meet new people and wake up to the birds singing! This is definitely not a good weather camp!

I remember lots of adventures at Girl Guide Camps in my teens in the 1970's. I learnt to pitch a ridge tent for the first time. A basic A-frame tent with heavy wooden poles and robust wooden pegs! No inner lining or integrated groundsheet in those days! We securely pitched the tent, tensioning the guy line ropes. Tent pegs are the most important of all the camping gear, together with a mallet to drive them down at a 45-degree angle!

We were safe and protected against the elements! So, what happened to my tent at the Grapevine Celebration on that stormy night? Some guy ropes had come off the pegs. The tent looked dishevelled in the morning, but it stayed up! No sleep, but all was well anchored to the ground. I reflected on the importance of fixing tent pegs securely!

Over the years, God showed me His Word is like those tent pegs. Firm and secure; solid, and when there were severe gales and storms in our lives, the *pegs* held us secure. Similarly, washing on a washing line on a windy day is held firm by the pegs!

God's promises are blood bought and rock solid. His Word stands firm. We are anchored by His Word. Storms may come and buffet us or try to move us, but we remain steadfast and immoveable; clinging

READY...GO!

to God's Word. Modern pop-up tents are not always fixed down with tent pegs; they can be quickly blown away! We need those pegs. We need God's Word in us so we can be grounded in Him every day. If you want to know God's will, read His Word! It leads, guides and encourages us. It has authority. It helps us to make good choices and decisions as we obey His commands:

"Your Word is a lamp to my feet, and a light to my path."

Psalm 119:105 (NKJV).

"Great peace have those who love your law, and nothing causes them to stumble."

Psalm 119:165 (NKJV).

Read the Word until you meet the Word! The living God. Speak God's Word into situations. His power goes with it. God spoke the universe into being! "Let there be light!" We can speak as He does; we have that authority in Him. It is good to have a daily habit of reading the Word. You can read it out loud, memorise it, pray it and meditate on it. Ask God to speak through His Word.

I enjoy listening to God's Word on audio, sometimes. Recently, I was challenged to read larger chunks of the Word and I had a day listening to the whole of the Psalms on audio! It was refreshing; I felt renewed and cleansed! The word has power to transform us. It brings joy, peace and hope. It contains the power of God to do His work and fulfil the promises of His Word. Speak God's Word over your life, other's lives and situations.

"For as the rain comes down, and the snow from heaven, and do not return there, but water the earth, and make it bring forth and bud, that it may give seed to the sower and bread to the eater, so shall My word be that goes forth from My mouth; it shall not return to Me

READY...GO!

void, but it shall accomplish what I please, and it shall prosper in the thing for which I sent it."

Isaiah 55:10-11 (NKJV).

God's Word is seed. The spreading of the Gospel and the expansion of the Kingdom life within us, both multiply by the seed of God's Word. Faith comes by hearing the word of God, by receiving it wholeheartedly. Fruitfulness is the guaranteed by-product, whether for the salvation of a lost soul, or the provision of a disciple's need. God's Word cannot be barren!

"Blessed is the man whose delight is in the law of the Lord, and on his law, he meditates day and night. He is like a tree planted by streams of water, which yields its fruit in season, and whose leaf does not wither. Whatever he does prospers."

Psalm 1:2-3 (NIV).

We can stand firm, overcome adversity and defeat temptation. Write out some of the promises of God that particularly speak to you. Proclaim them! Declare them over your life or circumstances. There is Power in the Word:

_____

_____

_____

_____

_____

_____

_____

READY...GO!

Chapter 34

Carry the Fire!

Camp fires are a wonderful end-of-day finale at Guide Camp! A time for singing, games, joy and relaxation. We sat in a circle feeling the warmth around the fire after a busy day. We collected sticks and twigs to add to the fire pit, then bigger chunks of wood. We listened to the crackle and fizz of the fire, as tall orange flames sent leaping sparks into the night sky. Pans suspended on home-made wooden tripods, heated milk for our hot chocolate and we toasted marshmallows in the flames. Wonderful!

Fire is a powerful symbol in the Bible. Fire purifies, destroys, consecrates, propels and welds together. Fire is a symbol of God's love, and the transforming power of the Holy Spirit. Moses met God in a flame of fire in the burning bush. Here, He recommissioned Moses to deliver a message to Pharaoh: *"Let My people go!"* God had seen their suffering and called Moses to lead the Israelites out of Egypt and into Canaan. In spite of reservations and doubts, Moses obeyed. God chooses to work through us, but *He* does the work of deliverance.

I like watching the Olympic flame in the torch relay heralding the start of the Olympic Games. The flame burns during the games until the closing ceremony when it is extinguished. We carry the fire, revival fire! We carry the baton. It cannot stop. God has His plans! The fire of God gives power to live. It equips and gives boldness. Fire welds us together in one accord; in unity. Fire purifies. The oldest method for purifying gold in the crucible is to melt it with fire. Our beautiful Refiner looks at us until He can see His face. Fire propels as in an engine room. Prayer and love stoke the fire and advance the Kingdom. At a camp fire, we warmed ourselves and drew near; many will come and sit by the fire to receive life and healing in His Presence.

READY...GO!

"He makes His servants flames of fire."

Hebrews 1:7 (NIV).

When we lay down our lives for God, we carry His Presence and fire. Fresh surrender, fresh fire! We let go of the old ways and structures that no longer carry His life and anointing. God hates a lukewarm church, one that compromises with the world:

"I know your deeds, that you are neither cold nor hot. I wish you were either one or the other! So, because you are lukewarm, neither hot nor cold, I am about to spit you out of My mouth."

Revelation 3:15-16 (NIV).

Jesus invites us to stir up faith and passion. He will come in blessing, power and fire.

As I wrote this poem I was assured of God's love. He wants us to walk closely with Him; often through the *fire*.

The Lord is close to the pure in heart,
He is always so close by,
He guides you; He is all your strength,
He hears your faintest sigh.

He leads you on the upward Way,
He takes you by the hand,
Though the path be rough and steep,
You see the Promised Land.

He says: "My child, be patient,
I know your heart's desire,
To move in oneness with the Son,
Though, now you see the fire.

READY...GO!

Walk in the light and praise your God,
Rest secure in Me,
Fix your eyes on Me alone,
The Way of the Kingdom you'll see."

Living stones together are built
Joined by His love,
Each one a chosen precious jewel
Reflecting that one above.

Fire births a move of God. How are you experiencing God's fire in your life?

_____
_____
_____
_____
_____
_____
_____

READY...GO!

Chapter 35

Why do you Lurk in the Shadows?

Children like to see their own shadows on a sunny day, and often chase each other's shadows! They find it funny to see a really short or very long shadow, as the angle of the sun changes! The Lord is showing me a *picture* of a cross. It casts a long shadow. I hear Him saying, "No lurking in the shadows!" I wrote a poem to capture God's heart. He reaches out, drawing us close to Him once again, to the cross:

"Why do you lurk in the shadows?
Surely the Way is clear,
The Cross speaks forgiveness and cleansing within,
Freedom from all fear.

Why then do you stay at a distance,
And wander around in the night?
See the shadow; it will not suffice,
Come into the glorious light.

Come to Me, My little child,
In whom I take delight,
I long that you would know my love,
Stay close in the darkest night.

Cast aside your earthly cares,
Come to the Cross of life,
See there I bore your infirmities,
Delivered you from this world's strife.

I am your life, says the Lord Most High,
Rest secure in Me,
Step out in faith, reach out in love,
Your heart's desire you will surely see."

READY…GO!

Sometimes, it seems like we're in the shadows. Maybe the shadows are somewhere dark where we are hiding in fear. God calls us to come into the light. He is light; there is no darkness in Him. He never changes. We can trust Him more deeply; He is the source of all good in our lives.

"Every good and every perfect gift is from above, and comes down from the Father of lights, with whom there is no variation or shadow of turning."

James 1:17 (NKJV).

When we are willing to consider the active will of God for our lives, we come to a personal knowledge of the Cross. Sometimes painful, but always fruitful! These are times where God draws us close to Himself.

"Until the day breaks and the shadows flee away, I will go my way to the mountain of myrrh and to the hill of frankincense."

Song of Songs 4:6 (NKJV).

In that place God changes us, and transforms us.

"Who is this coming up from the wilderness, leaning upon her beloved?"

Song of Songs 8:5 (NKJV).

She is not recognisable as she comes up from the wilderness, but transformed as she emerges leaning on her beloved. I don't want to be lurking in the shadows in any area of my life. God is calling us to come closer to Him, into the light and place of freedom.

READY...GO!

"But whoever lives by the truth comes into the light, so that it may be seen plainly that what he has done has been done through God."

John 3:21 (NKJV).

Is God speaking to you about any area in your life? Come out of the shadows into the light and write your thoughts below:

_____
_____
_____
_____
_____
_____
_____

READY...GO!

Chapter 36

Footprints in the Snow

On a cold, shivery, winter day, all was quiet and peaceful. A newly laid snow blanket stretched out in front of me. The air was fresh and crisp. Tiny tracks appeared in the snow. A bird left it's prints in a trail as he searched for food. Delicate arrowhead patterns left their mark.

Now, it's my turn! I heard the crunch beneath my boots as I made tracks in the clean snow. So satisfying to create fresh footprints! In time, the snow melted all the tracks, and all footprints disappeared; gone forever. I contemplated what mark I'd leave when I am no longer on this planet.

As I take steps each day, what footprints do I leave behind? What footprints do I want to leave? What is my legacy? Life on earth is no dress rehearsal. This is it; when it's gone, it's gone! Few of us will be remembered in this world beyond several generations.

> **What matters is to leave a legacy of character and faith that counts for eternity.**

Plant seeds in a garden you never get to see! Sow prayer, fasting and intercession; share the Good News of Salvation. Stand firm and live in faith in partnership with God and His church. In the end, all that will be left of importance will be what I did for God. So, while it is day, sow seeds that result in an eternal harvest. The only thing you can take to Heaven with you are souls. No seeds planted; no harvest! An obvious statement, but worth pointing out!

READY...GO!

"Do you not say, "Four months more and then the harvest?" I tell you, open your eyes and look at the fields! They are ripe for harvest."

John 4:35 (NIV).

I often say to myself "If not now, when?" and "If not me, who?" It keeps me on track!

"As long as it is day, we must do the work of Him who sent me. Night is coming when no-one can work."

John 9:4 (NIV).

Jesus had a finite amount of time to work in His earthly ministry. So, we as Christian believers have our earthly lives to accomplish the work of God He assigned to us. There is a sense of urgency. Time is short. Jesus is coming back to this earth; the second coming. No-one knows when; it will be as a thief in the night. All believers will be *caught up and raptured to meet the Lord in the air, in reference to 1 Thessalonians 4:16-17.*

The bodies of dead believers will be resurrected, and all believers, living and dead, will have glorified bodies. He will take His followers to live with Him in His wonderful Presence forever. The second coming is a fearful day for unbelievers, but a day of rejoicing and peace for those who believe and are saved. Don't get left behind. God loves you! He wants you to accept His gift of Salvation.

"The Lord is not slow in keeping His promise as some understand slowness. He is patient with you, not wanting anyone to perish, but everyone to come to repentance."

2 Peter 3:9 (NIV).

READY...GO!

I hear the Lord saying, "Let My love be the motivation, the power and strength interwoven in all you do. You will succeed! Walk closely with Me in My footsteps. Success is what is on My heart for you. What I am calling you to do will not fail. Love never fails." Let my footprints and legacy be love in its widest, highest and deepest way!

Consider your footprints. What are you leaving behind as you GO?
_____
_____
_____
_____
_____
_____

READY...GO!

Chapter 37

The River is Here

A breath-taking, spectacular view of the Rhine River opened up in front of me on the borders of Switzerland and Germany, ready for a boat ride up to the Rhine Falls. We put on our life jackets as we stepped into the boat and moved into the deep. A roaring sound got louder and louder, as the Falls came into view. It is deafening, though somehow soothing and calming too; drowning out all other noise! Water was plummeting into a plunge pool below. The spray on us was exhilarating, the largest waterfall in Europe! The boat tucked right into the side of the cascading, white waters. The power and motion were awe-inspiring. The continuous moving of the water, the flow of energy and life in the river was captivating.

Rivers have always been important to support life, to carry fresh water to people, plants and animals across the earth. Much loved places of relaxation and sports! A river always finds a way to go around or over obstacles. It never stops! There is a theme through the Bible from Genesis to Revelation of the River of God. This beautiful thread shows God's faithfulness and restoration. What is the river of God? It is the flowing out of God Himself; it brings life. In Genesis, when Adam and Eve sinned in the Garden of Eden, they no longer had access to the tree of life, and the river which is the source. There are incidences of water breaking through physically as the Bible unfolds. Moses experienced miraculous provision where the water poured out:

"The Lord said to Moses, "Take the staff, and you and your brother Aaron, gather the assembly together. Speak to that rock before their eyes and it will pour out its water. You will bring water out of the rock for the community so they and their livestock can drink."

Numbers 20:8 (NIV).

READY...GO!

It *pours* out, it isn't a trickle! There is a river in the prophetic vision of Isaiah; the outpouring of the Holy Spirit. Again, it's poured out! Abundance of water on the thirsty land:

"For I will pour water on the thirsty land and streams on the dry ground; I will pour out My Spirit on your offspring, and my blessing on your descendants."

Isaiah 44:3 (NIV).

In his vision, Ezekiel sees a life-giving river coming out from the Temple in reference to Ezekiel 47:1-12. As it flows, it grows in depth and width, giving life and fruitfulness to everything it touches, and healing. Where it flows into the Dead Sea, the water becomes fresh. *"Where the river flows, everything will live." (V9).*

Ankle deep, knee deep, waist deep; deep enough to swim! Let's get our feet off the bottom and swim in all God is pouring out today. We see the river in Jesus' ministry and He invites us to drink. Beautiful, pure, life-giving waters. *Come:*

"Jesus stood and said in a loud voice, "If anyone is thirsty, let him come to Me and drink. Whoever believes in Me, as the Scripture has said, streams of living water will flow from within him." By this, He meant the Spirit whom those who believed in Him were later to receive."

John 7:37 (NIV).

Fountains are open on the Cross. Jesus' Blood is that precious fountain to cover our sin.

"One of the soldiers pierced Jesus' side with a spear, bringing a sudden flow of blood and water."

John 19:34 (NIV).

READY...GO!

The Blood saves us from death; the water of the Holy Spirit flows from His side to bring life and restoration. As believers, we are temples of the Holy Spirit. The river flows on into Christian history; the river lost since Eden is regained in Christ. God's plans cannot be thwarted. The river never runs dry!

I hear the Lord calling, "See, a deluge is coming! You are My channel; swim, the speed of the current propels you. Do not be afraid. My Spirit is strong in you. Cling to Me. Everything else is swept away. My power is made perfect in weakness."

So, the beautiful river flows from Genesis to Revelation. We can have those streams of living waters flowing within us and *through* us today! If you are thirsty, come to Jesus and drink!

"For the Lamb who is in the midst of the throne will shepherd them and lead them to living fountains of waters. And God will wipe every tear from their eyes."

Revelation 7:17 (NKJV).

Drink deep of the life-giving waters. How is the river here for you today?

_____

_____

_____

_____

_____

_____

_____

READY...GO!

Chapter 38

Dismantle

A bricked up ancient doorway, God reveals His heart to me. The doorway seemed to be an opening that has long been closed. It is completely bricked up, yet He wants to take us through the door! He invites us to come. I see the brightness of His Presence coming through in cracks around the edges:

"Lift up your heads, Oh you gates! And be lifted up, you everlasting doors! And the King of Glory shall come in. Who is this King of Glory? The Lord, strong and mighty; the Lord mighty in battle."

Psalm 24:7-8 (NKJV).

> **He wants to take us where we've never been before. He wants to lead us in battle.**

I see a dismantling of all the bricks, one by one, steadily; each one is discarded. I see a word on each brick that He is showing me. A hindrance that needs dealing with and dismantling. What has kept us shut out? Maybe low self-esteem, depression, rejection, offence, worry, fear and unforgiveness.

New levels of chains are breaking. Are you tired of where you are? Come against every resistance hindering you from moving forwards. Confess any sins and come into repentance. Proclaim the truth of God's Word over each obstacle, each *brick* blocking the doorway. Tear down anything that empowers control; in other words, what man has built.

READY…GO!

The breaker-anointing shatters wrong agreements and partnerships. It opens the heavens and removes blockages that prevent the Presence of God from moving in fullness. Bricks are dismantled. In our lives and over regions and nations, we remove veils over our eyes and uproot stubborn roots. Like a battering ram with prayer and fasting, we see God's deliverance. We receive fresh oil and activate the breaker anointing.

"One who breaks open the way will go up before them; they will break through the gate and go out. Their king will pass through before them, the Lord at their head."

Micah 2:13 (NIV).

The original intention of an archway as a door, is to go in and out! When you totally surrender to God, He opens Heaven's resources for you. Every lie, bondage and obstacle must go! Jesus is looking for a family of restored ones who know who they are, who carry His heart, and who are partnering with Him to see His Kingdom come on earth. The doors open for new opportunities and greater influence for the Gospel.

"See, I have set before you an open door, and no one can shut it."

Revelation 3:8 (NKJV).

You have access to the Holy of Holies previously restricted to the High Priest. We can enter through the precious Blood of Jesus.

"Jesus said: "I am the door. If anyone enters by Me, he will be saved and will go in and out and find pasture."

John 10:9 (NKJV).

READY…GO!

There is an invitation to come. God won't drag us through the doorway! Praise takes us into His Presence and brings His Glory down. Let's walk through the door. There is a great dismantling! God is giving new mantles. We lay down our familiar, well-worn, old cloaks and mantles that hide who we really are.

God releases new mantles to fulfil our specific call and purpose in life. A mantle is a calling, a ministry and anointing given by God. Elijah anoints Elisha to succeed him as a prophet of God. Elijah wore a mantle; a cloak made of cloth. The passing of the mantle from Elijah to Elisha symbolises the passing of prophetic authority to Elisha in reference to 1 Kings 19:19. A mantle represents empowerment, sacrifice and commitment.

> **Elisha was willing to give up his security to obey the prophetic call. He acted on his faith, responded immediately with determination, to never look back.**

As believers, we all have gifts, mantles, and anointings for fruitfulness. As we pass through the doorway into God's Presence in total surrender, God will use us in tremendous ways.

"Each one should use whatever gift he has received to serve others faithfully administering God's grace in its various forms."

1 Peter 4:10 (NIV).

Are there any 'bricks' that need dismantling in your life so you can enter in to the fullness of God's Presence and what He has prepared for you?

_____

_____

_____

READY...GO!

READY...GO!
Chapter 39
A New Generation Rises

It was six months since leaving employment at a local children's nursery. I stepped in as a relief worker on my first day back. Walking around the playground, I saw a group of children with spades in their hands, wearing wellies and waterproofs, digging holes in the garden! My first thought was, "Are they allowed to do this?" There were no other adults in sight. I was wondering whether I should stop them! I looked a bit closer and there were lots of holes in the ground over a large area.

Six months ago, when I was last at my nursery, it was neat with well cut grass. It is now a vast expanse of mud like a building site! A small group of children, mostly 3-year-olds, were enthusiastically engaged in much activity. They filled the wheelbarrow with soil to fill in old holes and were digging new ones with great focus! I decided that it is alright for them to continue, purely for the amazing initiative they were showing! I remained a fascinated onlooker and watched them having fun. They were busily working together with purpose, different to anything I'd seen before!

I feel God is highlighting something here, and began to write it down. I heard the Lord speaking: "Do not say, *'this isn't how it used to be,'* comparing it to six months ago when the lawn was growing, neat and tidy! No! See what I am doing with a new generation; a new thing, even new assignments for the children. It is a new day as believers! Rise up. Do not look to the past.

For too long, My people have wanted a neat and tidy church that is contained. Will you be part of this new day and dig new ground? Fill in some holes, past ventures and past successes. Work in unity and harmony. What was once neat and tidy is now a building site, seemingly disorganised and chaotic, but the Kingdom is advancing! I bring change, but not for change sake, but to house my Glory; My Presence. Build in My way according to My pattern."

READY...GO!

I had the privilege that day in nursery to see "prophetic play" acted out! God is filling in old ways of doing things and traditions. This is now the time for new purposes to arise. The children I saw were definitely immersed in the moment. We too can move with a childlike trust. I hear God saying, "I want My Church back." What is He requiring of us?

> **Who we are and what we build is a reflection of God.**

We want to accurately reflect Jesus who is our pattern. I remember at school in needlework, making clothes from a pattern! We need a pattern. Seek God for His revelation and step out in obedience to uproot the familiar. Heart preparation for change and flexibility are key.

Let's ask God to purify our hearts and let Him work in us what He desires to do. It will pass the test of time if we build with *"gold, silver and precious stones, not wood, hay or straw."* In reference to *1 Corinthians 3:12-13*

Build *"according to the pattern."* God's words to Moses says:

"And let them make Me a sanctuary that I may dwell among them. According to all that I show you; that is, the pattern of the tabernacle and the pattern of all its furnishings, just so you shall make it."

Exodus 25:8-9 (NKJV).

The tabernacle was a tent or dwelling place that was sacred, dedicated to God for His Presence. God gave the Israelites the pattern or precise plans for its construction and furnishings. Verse 9 says: *"See to it that you make them according to the pattern which was shown you on the mountain."* Moses is told 3 times to *"follow*

READY...GO!

the pattern according to all I will show you." Give us listening ears, Lord, to hear Your voice and do what you are saying.

We cannot presume to know how God wants us to build.

"There is a way that seems right to a man, but its end is the way of death."

Proverbs 16:25 (NKJV).

Let's not build according to the former patterns. Make way for the new! Let's champion the children and youth of today as we pray and encourage them to step into everything God has for them and move on together!

Is God giving you a "pattern" for something in your life?

_____
_____
_____
_____
_____
_____
_____

READY…GO!

Chapter 40

Treasure to Share!

GO! Tell the world of the treasure you have found!

I heard the Lord saying, "I am your treasure. You are full and overflowing; a treasure chest in Me. You have much to give away. You are one who displays My Glory. Many come and taste and eat. You provide food for many. The treasure chest never becomes empty. As you give, so I pour out My abundant supplies. You are never lacking. See, if I will not open the windows of heaven and rain down gifts, much to give away, to touch lives around you. Step into new pathways of trust and fruitfulness. Go with precious seed to sow. I will multiply it!"

It may be that you don't yet have an assurance of God's amazing love for you personally. He is waiting with open arms. He loves you. Come to Him. You can pray the salvation prayer from the Introduction and give your life to God today. It is the best decision you can ever make. Run into all that God has for you and your family. Tell others of your decision to follow Jesus. Meet with other believers, grow in the pursuit and intimacy of your relationship with God and let Him reveal what He wants you to do. The truth of God's word will radically transform your life as you know who you are *in* Christ Jesus.

I have an old piece of paper in my Bible with these words written on it: "What makes you come alive? Do it! Not, what does the world need? The world needs people who have come alive through the knowledge of His Will." Maybe they were some notes from a sermon many years ago; I'm not sure, but they are priceless!

If you've had negative experiences of church, reach out again. The Body of Christ needs you. Through years of trials and difficulties, God has deposited much treasure in you! Your history doesn't define your destiny. We are called to belong to God's family and share in

READY…GO!

Christ's mission to the world. Fix your eyes on Jesus. We are created to serve God in the church, and in mission to the world. Sow the seed. *Do not despise the day of small things*, in reference to Zechariah 4:10. It may seem tiny, but the repercussions are massive! Revival may start small, but a seed is powerful. Sow generously whatever you have. Sow the Gospel. Revival is here, now!

"As you GO, preach, saying, 'The Kingdom of Heaven is at hand.' Heal the sick, cleanse the lepers, raise the dead, cast out demons. Freely you have received, freely give."

Matthew 10:7-8 (NKJV).

Sow kindness, encouragement, finances, prayer, fasting, work, love, joy, peace, time and much more. Let God work in you and through you. Whatever you have in your hand, give it joyfully and look for the 100-fold increase! What we do now impacts eternity. *"Press on to take hold of that for which Christ Jesus took hold of you."* Philippians 3:12. (NIV)

At nursery, I took a child's hand as they positioned themselves to jump from a high-climbing block. I say **'READY…GO!'** They took a leap! We have confidence in Christ and the assurance that He is with us. He says to us **'READY…GO!'** Let us step into all He has planned for us, with courage and joy!

"Be strong and of good courage; do not be afraid, nor dismayed, for the Lord your God is with you wherever you go."

Joshua 1:9 (NKJV).

Don't wait for anyone to give you permission to fulfil the call of God on your life. You are commissioned today!

READY…GO!

READY...GO!

Jesus said: "Peace to you! As the father has sent Me, I also send you."

John 20:21 (NKJV).

Reflect on the words READY...GO. What do they mean to you? Write your thoughts on what has particularly inspired you the most:

_____
_____
_____
_____
_____
_____
_____
_____

www.ingramcontent.com/pod-product-compliance
Lightning Source LLC
Chambersburg PA
CBHW020426010526
44118CB00010B/435